Ask the
Old Football Coach

Ask the Old Football Coach

Brilliantly Brainless Advice
from the Ghosts of Gridiron Past

Jesse Farrar

Guilford, Connecticut

An imprint of Globe Pequot

Distributed by NATIONAL BOOK NETWORK

British Library Cataloguing in Publication Information available

Library of Congress Cataloging-in-Publication Data available

ISBN 978-1-4930-3007-1 (hardback)
ISBN 978-1-4930-3006-4 (e-book)

∞™ The paper used in this publication meets the minimum requirements of American National Standard for Information Sciences—Permanence of Paper for Printed Library Materials, ANSI/NISO Z39.48-1992.

Printed in the United States of America

Introduction

The casual professional football fan, of which there are evidently hundreds of millions, has no idea what a hypocrite he is. Despite devoting virtually no thought at all to the inner workings, backroom deals, and contractual complexities that make his Sunday afternoon prostrate beer-guzzling a socially acceptable pastime, he fancies himself a total fanatic of the local team, and spends an inordinate amount of money every year on baubles expressing same.

That may well be true of most of us. If it didn't explicitly occur on the field, between our trips to the bathroom, it may as well not have happened. Unlike basketball, baseball, or hockey, whose devotees may rattle off at the drop of a hat a few obscure playoff conventions or the finer points of the CBA, many NFL fans would be hard-pressed to recite the current standard for a completed pass. Football may very well be number one in our hearts—for now at least—but we tend to keep much of the game itself, from rulebook to playbook, at a stiff arm's length. I think I understand why.

The game that used to exist only on Ivy League school quads and far-flung radio broadcasts is long dead. That game, like the one we know and love today, was random, cruel, and unapologetically violent. But, unlike the primetime ratings bonanza now foisted upon America three times a week, the football of the past was largely unloved. It was also unpolished, amateurish, dull, unoriginal, and nearly invisible to most of the country, which is not coincidental.

Within that context, turning on a contemporary edition of NBC's *Sunday Night Football*, say, and bearing witness to the sparkling sheen of professionalism and focus-grouped marketing that's been pasted over the pockmarked surface of the sport *per se* is, in a word, utterly discombobulating. To wit, in what sense should we understand the glamorous new arena, miles away from its two-decade-old "dilapidated" predecessor, in a sprawling "Coming Soon!" mixed-use suburban oasis, financed largely by the working-class fans who can no longer afford to attend events there, to have been "sold out"?

Or at what point do we stop rooting for players based on which college received between two to six years of their unpaid, high-risk labor in exchange for a meal plan and exposure, and start rooting for players based on which modern-day robber baron's father paid a nominal franchise fee in the county closest to where we were born? And if players are terminated midway through their contract for using drugs that help them maintain a competitive edge, heal more rapidly, or cope with the damage they do to their bodies every day, are we still their fans?

Maybe you have the time and mental bandwidth to consider these and more conundrums while you watch, dear reader, or perhaps not. But regardless, by an overwhelming margin, you *are* still watching despite it all, and the NFL knows it. Efforts to redress the important social issues plaguing the game, the league, and the general broadcast experience will therefore be token at best. More likely, these issues will be exacerbated.

But still, we watch. Why?

Consider these words from John Heisman, widely considered to be one of football's most influential architects:

> *We all know that by collegians the game is esteemed the king of sports, and it deserves no less ranking, for it has the power to create and to arouse "college spirit" as does nothing else from one end of the campus to another. Now college spirit is a*

mighty fine thing. It teaches the meaning of the words loyalty, fidelity, love of country, patriotism.

There you have it. Despite all the grifting, the commercialization, and the ground-up human capital, we never miss a game because, at the end of the day, we are insane. We're completely, undeniably, swinging-a-dead-cat-around-in-a-parking-lot-and-hollering-level bonkers, with no intention to get better and no conceivable remedy. True nutjobs!

Only the truly insane, after all, would see patriotism in a sport that is regularly compensated by the military to "salute the troops" before games, or loyalty in a league that forcibly drafts its talent. (Admittedly, the fidelity of the artificially piped-in crowd noise is decent, but whatever.) More to the point, these values reflect the undeniably ill-informed, genteel, and superstitious worldview shared by, wouldn't you know it, basically every football coach and player ever.

Luckily for us, many of these influential men . . . these fearless trailblazers . . . these bigtime dummies if you will (and if you won't, I will) had the foresight to codify their thoughts in an easily roasted and riffable format during the short window in history that would legally allow their inane goofball rants to be reprinted without permission. So without further ado, I am now going to do that. Please enjoy.

P.S. If you happen to find your work in the pages to come, I am deeply sorry. Tell your great grandchildren to roast this book when I am dead.

HARVARD

On Calling the Plays

It seems a very simple matter to say that the receiver should be called *before* the pass is made to him. It seems so simple that time is rarely spent in practicing it. . . . The usual thing is for the passer to hurl the ball into the air and yell "ball." Let any coach actually insist once on his passer calling his man *before* he passes to him and see what happens. And yet this is exactly the thing that will change the forward pass game from a happy-go-lucky chance into a mathematical probability. When the passer calls his man *before* he passes he knows what he is trying to do, the team knows, the receiver is given more time to get into position, he is then given a better chance to catch the pass.

Elmer Berry, *The Forward Pass in Football*, 1921

Yeah, and you could also maybe have the receiver wear a special flashing jersey that says "He's going to throw the ball to me for sure!"

COLLIER'S
SPORTING
NUMBER
EDWARD PENFIELD

On Trickery

To show to what extremes unscrupulous coaches will go, the following incident, which actually took place during a game, will suffice. At the beginning of the second half, the team whose turn it was to receive the kickoff took position with only ten men in uniform. The eleventh player, dressed in civilian attire, which included derby hat and pipe, was naturally not observed by opponents or officials, as he casually paced up and down the sidelines. After the kickoff was run back, on the first play from scrimmage, a forward pass was thrown to this individual, who meanwhile had stepped within the field of play and thus complied with all the requisites of the rules. Being totally unaware of his presence as a player, the defense naturally left unprotected the territory in his vicinity, with the result that he ran some forty yards before he was overtaken.

Percy H. Haughton, *Football, and How to Watch It*, 1922

"The Pipe Smoker's Gambit," as it later became known, was as devastating as it was effete and pretentious.

On Popularity

TO FOOTBALL

Farewell to thee, Cricket,
Thy last match is o'er;
Thy bat, ball, and wicket
Are needed no more.
To thy sister we turn,
For her coming we pray;
Her worshippers burn
For the heat of the fray.
Hail! Goddess of battle,
Yet hated of Ma(r)s,
How ceaseless their tattle
Of tumbles and scars!
Such warnings are vain,
For thy rites we prepare,
Youth is yearning again
In thy perils to share.
Broken limbs and black eyes
May, perchance, be our lot;
But grant goals and ties
And we care not a jot.
Too sacred to name
With thy posts, ball, and field,
There is no winter game
To which thou canst yield.

Mr. Punch's Book of Sport,
edited by J. A. Hammerton, 1910

Nothing says "Let's get ready to play some contact sports!" quite like an ABAB rhyme scheme.

On Fun

When thirty thousand people are willing to forsake comfortable homes and profitable business to sit several hours upon boards in chill November winds to witness a football game between rival colleges, no one can doubt that the game is eminently successful as an entertainment. Few persons who know the game will deny that, also, it has excellent qualities as sport, for "sport" and "entertainment" are by no means equivalent terms.

George E. Merrill, *Is Football Good Sport?*, 1903

And if you don't believe that, just ask a Browns fan.

On Business

The making of a football team . . . is not unlike the making of a miniature army. The recruiting officer is at the gymnasium, where every candidate must pass a severe physical examination before he is allowed to take part in the sport. He is then sent to the field and put in the hands of the drill sergeant to be made or broken. If he is one of the eleven best men among three thousand, he is then attached to his regiment, the eleven. The organization, equipment, management, and direction of this little army, which fights for the glory of school, college, or university, is under many bureaus conducted upon strictly business principles.

William H. Lewis, "Making a Football Team,"
Outing Volume XLI, 1903

Well, except there's no job security, pay, or benefits, and once you join, it's nearly impossible to leave. Also, if you get bad grades you're fired and your boss will insult you on national television. Other than that, though . . . college football is strictly business, baby.

On Officiating

Any man who is willing to undertake the responsibilities of a referee must first be certain that he knows all the laws down to their minutest details. . . . He will be wise to carry a rule-book in his pocket, both for the purpose of refreshing his own memory before the match begins, and of convincing any captain who questions his interpretations on the field. We hold that every player should read the laws before each season, but that a referee should study them before every match. It is only by constant study that a referee can hope to be prompt with his decisions; and unless a decision is given promptly it loses half its effect.

Poe's Football: How to Play the Most Popular Amateur Game, 1904

The idea of officials taking exorbitant amounts of time to make a call, thereby eroding significantly their authority among players and fans alike is hypothetically too absurd to consider, even for a moment!

On Treats

As I told you in the first chapter, a player should not smoke. Neither, I might add, should he take alcohol. While pastries are bad for him, yet, as a dessert he may have a little ice cream and occasionally a simple sweet pudding. As a matter of fact, any player who watches himself closely can pretty well tell for himself what does and does not agree with him.

Walter Camp, *Football Without a Coach*, 1920

A player shouldn't have candy! Well, all right, maybe he can have a little candy. Absolutely no pop, though. Oh, okay, he can drink some pop. But I swear on the cross if I see him eating just one morsel of my German dark chocolate, I'll . . . fine, he can eat all the chocolate! I don't care!

FOOTBALL

On Heroes of the Game

It is not my purpose to select an all-star football team from the long list of heroes past and present. It is not possible to select any one man whom we can all crown as king. We all have our football idols, our own heroes, men after whom we have patterned, who were our inspiration.

We can never line up in actual scrimmage the heroes of the past with those of more recent years. What a treat if this could be arranged!

There are many men I have idolized in football, not only for their record as players, but for the loyalty and spirit for the game which they have inspired.

William H. Edwards, *Football Days: Memories of the Game and of the Men behind the Ball*, 1916

It would rock if we could dig up all our old dead friends and ram their skulls together for a few hours. On account of how much we all respect them, or whatever.

On Safety

Even a short work on football would be unsatisfactory unless it devoted at least a few pages to the discussion of the commoner football injuries. Of course, broken bones, dislocated joints, internal injuries and such serious pathological conditions are for the expert surgeon to handle. Happily these are not nearly so frequent in occurrence as prior to 1903, when the game underwent sweeping rule changes in order to make it safer.

John W. Heisman, *Principles of Football*, 1922

Football: Completely Safe Since 1903.

On Visual Learning

It is impossible in a general article to go into all the details of this popular game. Many authors have tried to make the rules and the methods plain, but they have not succeeded very well. The best way to learn is from an old player or to watch old players at the game.

Alfred Rochefort, *Healthful Sports for Boys*, 1910

Another good way to learn would be from a writer who gives a damn. Oh well! Time to go enjoy all the fun stuff from 1910, such as rolling a hoop up a hill and waiting for it to come back down again.

On Body Types

The position of guard, while it requires less agility than that of tackle, can never be satisfactorily filled by a man who is slow. Many a coach makes this mistake and fails to see his error until too late to correct it. I remember once seeing upon a minor team a guard who weighed at least 190 pounds replaced by a man of 155, and the latter actually filled the position—greatly to my astonishment, I confess—in excellent fashion. This does not at all go to prove that weight is of no value in a guard. On the contrary, it is a quality especially to be desired, and if one can find a heavy man who is not slow he is the choice by all means.

Walter Camp, *American Football*, 1891

But if you can't find one of those guys, just put, like, a small lady or a kid on the line. Or a dog. Who cares, really. I'm so blasted on laudanum I don't even know who I am.

On the Viewers at Home

And watching the game in this vicarious manner isn't so bad as the fellow who has got tickets and carfare to the real game would like to have it. You are in a warm room, where you can stretch your legs and regulate your remarks to the intensity of your emotions rather than to the sex of your neighbors. And as for thrills! "Dramatic suspense" was probably first used as a term in connection with this indoor sport. The scene is usually some college club in the city—a big room full of smoke and graduates. At one end is a scoreboard and miniature gridiron, along which a colored counter is moved as the telegraph behind the board clicks off the plays hot from the real gridiron.

Robert Benchley, *Of All Things*, 1921

This experience sounds so much better than four hours' worth of instant replays and truck ads that it almost makes Prohibition seem workable.

The Eleven Jankiest Records of Pro Football Hall of Fame Coaches

- **Jimmy Conzelman (87-63-17)**
  Conzelman's coaching record, mediocre as it is, is perhaps most notable for being compiled while he was also playing for, managing, and in some cases, owning the very teams for whom he coached.
- **Weeb Ewbank (130-129-7)**
  He wouldn't have known it at the time, but if Ewbank hadn't ridden Joe Namath and his decidedly underdog New York Jets to a narrow victory in 1969's Super Bowl III, he would have gone on to end his Hall of Fame career with exactly as many losses earned as wins.
- **Sid Gillman (123-104-7)**
  Gillman is credited for both inventing, more or less, the modern passing game and conceiving of a merged super-league between the NFL and AFL. He is also the only coach to be enshrined in both the College and Pro Football Halls of Fame. That's all very impressive, but it does raise the question: Why did he lose so many damn games?
- **Bud Grant (168-108-5)**
  If you count CFL win-loss records, Bud Grant joins an esteemed club as one of the winningest coaches in professional football history. Needless to say, I do not count CFL win-loss records.
- **Marv Levy (154-120-0)**
  Because of his indelible association with the 1990-1993 Bills, there's a strong case to be made that Marv Levy is among the most infamous losers of all time. That he is a well-known Cubs fan who was in attendance for Chicago's lone successes spanning centuries of incompetence—I'm projecting into the future a bit here—is merely icing on the cake.
- **Walt Kiesling (30-55-5)**
  Well, Walt, you may have not-won exactly twice as many games as you won, but so long as you didn't bench and then cut one of the greatest quarterbacks of all time, you can be in the Hall of Fame. Oh, what the hell, you can still be in. We can't say no to you.

- **Bert Bell (10-46-2)**
  Bert Bell makes Dave Shula look like Don Shula. Also, genetics do that, too.
- **Steve Owen (155-108-17)**
  In 1934, Owen's NY Giants faced the defending champion and undefeated Chicago Bears juggernaut in the second NFL Championship Game at Polo Grounds in New York. The field was frozen and unforgiving, and the Giants faced a 10-3 deficit at halftime. The Ed Thorp Memorial Trophy seemed all but lost. That is, until Owen got his pals to swipe some sneakers from a local school's basketball team. With what in those days would have passed for winter-appropriate athletic wear, the Giants stormed back to win by a final tally of 30-13. This ingenious strategy, also known as cheating, is perhaps Owen's most enduring legacy.
- **Bill Parcells (183-138-1)**
  In a 1987 NYT profile, Parcells gives his explanation for the bizarre "Big Tuna" sobriquet:

  "When I was coaching with the Patriots," he said, "the players pulled a practical joke and I said, 'Do you think I'm Charlie the Tuna, like a sucker?' After that, they called me Tuna."

  It's complete nonsense, of course, as Parcells in fact earned the oceanic nom de plume after a chance encounter with an especially ornery fisherman's net.
- **Hank Stram (131-97-10)**
  It is often said that without Hank Stram, there would be no Gatorade. Or, at least, that's what he wants us to think. Meanwhile, he's free to rack up, like, a billion losses. We're on to you, Stram.
- **Guy Chamberlin (58-16-7)**
  At 78.4 percent, Chamberlin owns the second-highest winning percentage of any coach in NFL history with more than twenty-three games under his belt. That's pretty good—excellent, actually. But I'm leaving him on the list to justify a second printing of this book. For the actual eleventh jankiest record among HOF coaches and an erratum longer than an Andy Reid playbook, be sure to pick up all forthcoming editions of *Ask The Old Football Coach* in hardcover, paperback, softpaper, coversoft, audiopress, digi-book, and UltraDisk™.

On Spectacle

If one is interested in neither side, no game is more tedious to witness. Almost every time the ball touches the ground the game stops, the masses of armored legs are disentangled and time is given for those who have lost their breath to rise to their feet again. Once in a while a brilliant run stands out as a marked exception, but the interference which makes the run possible is often invisible to spectators. Of course if football were a true sport, this would be no objection, for a sport has its value in the delight of the players themselves and in their improved physical development. That which is played for the benefit of spectators is a spectacle, not a sport. And no man lives who would play the American game of football for pure sport, knowing that nobody would ever be on the bleachers and that neither his name nor that of his adversaries would resound among his fellows or appear in headlines in the newspapers. I honor the scrubs, those who play day after day that the first team may grow strong by running over them. This is the true college spirit, but there is no scrub who would play the American game for fun.

David Starr Jordan, *Football: Battle or Sport*, 1908

The only way this essay could have aged any worse is if it inexplicably beat out *The Shawshank Redemption* for Best Picture.

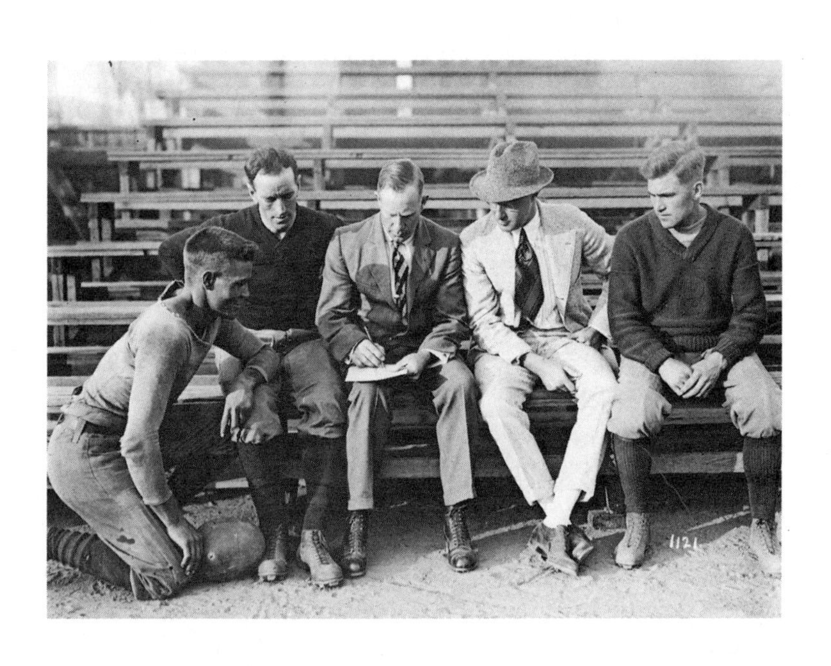
1121

On Assistants

Five assistant coaches are necessary. . . . More than seven assistants are bad. A large number of coaches produces an underdeveloped, characterless team. The coaches should be: one end coach, two line coaches, one back-field coach, one second-eleven coach. The position coaches make the team, by their work in position and group drill. . . . The limit on the number of coaches prescribed above is not meant to rule out special coaches for particular performances. It is always advisable to secure a good instructor, if available, for work on the specialties, such as drop kicking, goal kicking, and passing.

Charles D. Daly, *American Football*, 1921

Man, why don't you just figure out how many coaches we're supposed to have and then write the book when you're done.

BALL.
F.R.G.

On the Drop-Kick

It may be argued that the placement kick seems to involve the accuracy of two men instead of one only; but the placer need not be a wonder. If he be the quarterback, as probably is the case, he is already well accustomed to the handling of the ball from center; while the actual placing of the ball is an exceedingly simple assignment. The kicker, knowing precisely where the ball is to be placed, locates himself where a line from his advancing toe through the center of the ball will bisect the goal, if there is no wind. Like the drop-kicker, he must calculate the speed of his kick and its height, and make proper allowance for the wind. But his advantage over the drop-kicker in ability to control and regulate the direction and the angle of departure is positive. Prompt and decisive elevation on placement kicks can be acquired by anybody. Many drop-kicks, especially if driven hard in order to obtain distance, leave the ground at a low angle, and would assuredly strike one rush line or the other if kicked from five, or even seven, yards behind center.

Maj. Frank W. Cavanaugh, *Inside Football*, 1919

It's a good thing they spent all this time analyzing and perfecting drop-kicks, the element of the game we all love so much today.

On the Off-Tackle Run

There is nothing peculiar or extraordinary about this play. It is one of the simplest plays in the game and under a slightly different form used to be a standard play in the big schools before the days of the forward pass.

It is one of the best plays that can be devised, for after all no matter how complicated the formation or theory of attack, there are only so many avenues of attack. This is one of the strongest.

Ernest Graves and John J. McEwen,
Forty Winning Plays in Football, 1922

Forty Winning Plays was not just a book, but a business. These guys were selling their plays to teams around the country. "It's boring, simple, and old" is evidently how they sold this one. I wonder if it worked.

On Hurdling

So often does one hear the cry of "hurdling" from the grandstand, and so seldom is the hurdling penalty imposed immediately thereafter, that it is well worth while getting an accurate idea . . . of what hurdling as the officials understand it, really is. . . . [H]urdling in football is like hurdling on the track, a deliberate attempt to clear an obstacle by leaping when in full stride with the knee of the leg in advance well up, and quitting the stride for an instant for that purpose. [H]urdling in football is *not* striding or running over the bodies of prostrate opponents. Furthermore a player on one knee may be hurdled without penalty.

Herbert Reed, *Football for Public and Player*, 1913

Did people in 1913 really need the concept of a jump explained to them in this kind of detail? I know it was a different time and all, but it's just a jump, folks. Relax. Even bugs do it.

VOL. LXVI. No. 1706. PUCK BUILDING, New York, November 10th, 1909. PRICE TEN CENTS.

"What Fools these Mortals be!"

Puck

Entered at N. Y. P. O. as Second-class Mail Matter.

THE EASY UMPIRE

"He slugs me every chance he gets, and you can't or won't see it."

On The Captain's Duty To Appeal

The captain of a football team should know all the rules by heart—not only the rules of play, but also the rules governing umpires and referees, because with him lies the duty of making any necessary appeals and of sternly repressing all unwarrantable appeals on the part of his men. If this elementary precaution was taken by all captains we might hope to see less of the bickering and wrangling which are far too prevalent at the present time.

Poe's Football: How to Play the Most Popular Amateur Game, 1904

6 Traits Every Team Captain MUST Have:

Smart
Agile
Natural Leader
Sternly Repressing
Bookworm
No Wrangling

On Pacific Coast Football

In the championship series Stanford holds the balance of two games, though there is very little difference in the number of points scored. Stanford has won six games, California has won four, and four have been ties. . . .

Yet Stanford and California are by no means the only good teams in the field. Every year the University of Nevada produces an aggregation of husky sagebrushers who cause considerable anxiety to their larger rivals, and in past years have scored victories over both the Cardinal and the Blue and Gold.

H.L. Baggerly, *Spalding's Official Foot Ball Guide*, 1904

"An aggregation of husky sagebrushers who cause considerable anxiety"? Yeah, I saw those little guys the weekend I took that expired Mucinex. I think I beat up a Cardinal, too. That's what the warrant said, anyway.

On Quizzes

Quizzes on the rules should be held frequently early in the season, and not omitted late in the season. Insist, particularly, that the men learn the penalties. This is a very good way to teach the game, as a matter of fact, for there is a great deal of football wrapped up in the definitions of offenses, and players show at least a certain degree of curiosity to find out what may happen to them in case they do commit any forbidden action. But a few men at least on every squad will prove apt students and able football lawyers.

Maj. Frank W. Cavanaugh, *Inside Football*, 1919

Sherman, I've got some bad news: You got an F on the football quiz. Also, I've got some good news: I'm still going to let you throw the football tomorrow because I'm not a moron.

On the Five-Yard-Rule

If a team, using these tactics, should be forced behind its own goal line, the ball was taken out to the twenty-five-yard line and the same style of play resumed. This game could thus be prolonged indefinitely, and was used quite extensively during two or three seasons, after which two steps were taken to check it.

The first of these was to make a safety count two points against the side making it, and the second was to adopt the so called "five-yard-rule." The latter provided that a team holding the ball must, in three successive fairs or downs, advance it five yards or retreat with it twenty, and, failing to do this, must deliver it over to the other side.

Walter Camp and Lorin F. Deland, *Football*, 1896

When I was growing up, the "five-yard-rule" stipulated that if you threw some food and it only went five yards, you could still eat it. Most food is not very aerodynamic, so I was kind of a chubby kid.

JUNIOR

On, Uhh…

The display of suggestive pictures on the walls of students' rooms must be taboo with every man who is sincerely striving for the manly life, it matters not whether the pictures be in the guise of real art or not. The fact that a picture which tends to stimulate the imagination of men in dangerous directions is the work of a great master does not justify its presence in a student's room. Untold harm in the lives of the strongest of men is often done by so-called "works of art" in the nude. . . .

Last year a football star on one of the big teams, with one of the most important games approaching, was having seminal emissions every night. He and his coaches were very much concerned for it was taking the edge off his condition. Finally one of the coaches went to the player's room one evening and discovered a picture of a nude, female figure hanging on the wall at the foot of his bed. The coach tore it from the wall and lectured the fellow in no uncertain terms. A real cause of the abnormal emissions had been discovered.

M. J. Exner, MD, *The Rational Sex Life for Men*, 1914

"Coach, I'm horny!"

On the Rules of Catching

1. The commonest fault of a catcher is to go down field farther than he has been coached.
2. The next commonest is that he doesn't go in quite the right direction.
3. An ineligible man should try hard to avoid being touched by a passed ball.
4. If you can't catch it yourself bluff hard that you are trying to catch it—yet spoil it for opponents.
5. Be prepared instantly to tackle if an opponent gets it.
6. Don't fall on a pass that has grounded.

John W. Heisman, *Principles of Football*, 1922

"He doesn't catch the ball" just narrowly misses the cutoff, coming in as the 1,325th commonest fault of catchers. Fault number 1,324 being, of course, "He wakes up to find himself in a strange alien world and cannot return to Earth's dimension in time for the game."

ON EFFORT

It is a cardinal principle of the offense that the enemy must be licked; it can seldom be tricked into defeat. When plays are well mastered by constant, tireless drill and practise, and are brought in unison by the eleven, the coach next turns his attention to getting power and speed into the plays, to make each man put his weight, strength, skill, and quickness into the execution of every [maneuver]. This process is called "putting ginger" into the men, or putting spirit into the team, a most difficult thing in some cases, but very easy with men of the right temperament and disposition.

WILLIAM H. LEWIS, "MAKING A FOOTBALL TEAM,"
OUTING VOLUME XLI, 1903

"Get out there and lick those men or I'm going to stuff you full of ginger."

PRESS

On Egalitarianism

It is only natural that boys and young men who love a hard, clean game of physical prowess should select football. The beauty of the sport is that there seems to be a place on a football team for a player of any physique, provided, of course, that he is in normal health. The fat boy, who has been the joke of his comrades, suddenly finds that he is excellent material for a football center, provided—another of course—that he works hard and masters the position. The active little fellow, who has not been able to hold his own with the bigger boys in wrestling and other rough sports finds himself a quarterback through his ability to use his hands and his head. The big slow boy gets a place as guard, and the fast quick tracer goes out on the end. And the boy who can kick and forward pass finds a place for himself behind the line. There is room for all.

Walter Camp, *Football Without a Coach*, 1920

Football in this modern age of 1920 is for everybody! Except women, minorities, and people with disabilities. And nerds. And foreigners!

T.FREUND.

ON SIMILARITIES WITH SNOW BATTLES

Now, a snow battle . . . calls for that endurance and tact that distinguishes the true soldier. The two selected captains toss up in the usual manner for first choice of men. Then alternately, as in a spelling bee, each chooses a soldier until all are taken. The taw lines are then drawn, about thirty feet apart, and two flag staffs with colored handkerchiefs for flags are erected in each camp. To bear the enemy's flag to your own camp, that is, over the taw line, wins the victory for your side. Tackling is allowed, as in football. . . . No boy bearing the mark of a snowball on chest or back is allowed to take further part in the game, as he is considered to be a dead soldier. . . . No tripping, no striking, no ice balls, and no "soakers" (wet snowballs) are allowed.

A. R. CALHOUN, *HEALTHFUL SPORTS FOR BOYS*, 1910

All right, boys! No striking, no soakers, and anyone with a snowball on their back is dead, okay? Just like in the game of football, which, incidentally, I have never played.

FOOT
BALL
A
E. KidMAN '13.

On Predisposition

There is still another kind of football instinct, and that is the kind that is passed down from father to son and from brother to brother. They say that the lacemakers of Nottingham don't have to be taught how to make lace because, as children, they somehow absorb most of the necessary knowledge in the bosom of their family, and I think the same thing is true of sons and brothers of football players. Generally, they pick up the essentials of the game from "Pop" long before they get to school or college or else are properly educated by an argus-eyed brother.

William H. Edwards, *Football Days: Memories of the Game and of the Men behind the Ball*, 1916

I'm fairly sure even the lacemakers of Nottingham could figure out how to run in a straight line without immediately falling down. They probably know stuff other than lace. Kind of a weird thing to imply.

FOOTBALL
RULES
GEOMETRY
CHEMISTRY
ASKIN

On the Rules of Kicking

These rules were also adopted by the Board of Managers of the Amateur Athletic Union, June 2, 1888. Re-approved May 18, 1890.

Rule 1

(a) A drop-kick is made by letting the ball fall from the hands and kicking it at the very instant it rises from the ground.

(b) A place-kick is made by kicking the ball after it has been placed on the ground.

(c) A punt is made by letting the ball fall from the hands and kicking it before it touches the ground.

(d) Kick-off is a place-kick from the center of the fields of play, and cannot score a goal.

(e) Kick-out is a drop-kick by a player of the side which has touched the ball down in their own goal, or into whose touch-in-goal the ball has gone, and cannot score a goal.

(f) A free-kick is one where the opponents are restrained by rule.

Poe's Football: How to Play the Most Popular Amateur Game, 1904

And if you don't like these kicking rules, just wait around a bit. We pretty much change 'em every forty seconds.

ELLIMANIUS
EMBROCATIUS FOR
BRUSIUS

On Nicknames and Rough Play

The nicknames with which the Indians labelled each other were mostly those of animals or a weapon of defense. Mount Pleasant and Libby always called each other Knife. . . . Other names fastened to the different players were Whale Bone, Shoe String, Tommyhawk and Wolf.

The Indians always played cleanly as long as their opponents played that way. Dillon, an old Sioux Indian, and one of the fastest guards I ever saw, was a good example of this. If anybody started rough play, Dillon would say, "Stop that, boys!" and the chap who was guilty always stopped. But if an opponent continually played dirty football, Dillon would say grimly: "I'll get you!" On the next play or two . . . the rough player would be taken out. Dillon had "got" his man.

William H. Edwards, *Football Days: Memories of the Game and of the Men behind the Ball*, 1916

Then there was ol' Crossbow Johnson . . . what a card he was! And a hell of a kicker, too. Anyway, you'd have to watch yourself around ol' Crossbow, on account of he was a real stickler for his boys giving 100 percent effort. If Crossbow saw you runnin' slack or not givin' your all, sure enough, it wouldn't be too long till you were drug up outta the nearest body of water with a crossbow bolt sticking out of your ear.

On Beginnings

Football, or, as it was called in olden time, camp-ball, camping, or hurling, may be traced from the present backward through century after century until the trail is lost in the remoteness of antiquity. Indeed, abundant evidence may be marshalled to prove that this is the oldest outdoor game in existence.

Parke H. Davis, *Football: The American Intercollegiate Game*, 1917

Well, sure, if you ignore Bearball! Actually, you probably should ignore Bearball. A grim sport . . . not for the faint of heart.

On Pass Defense

There is no defense for the forward pass. . . .

Thus far most teams have trusted to luck against the forward passing game. The inefficiency and mechanical errors of its offense, aided by the restrictive legal measures adopted, have conspired to make this possible. Signs are not lacking, however, to indicate a greatly increased use of the passing game, an improved understanding and appreciation of its fundamental principles and a much greater degree of success for it. The defense for the forward pass will need to be studied with great care in the immediate future.

The writer does not pretend to have solved this problem. His interest has been rather on the other side. The following suggestions are offered simply as a beginning. . . .

Elmer Berry, *The Forward Pass in Football*, 1921

Apparently, all you had to do to get a book deal in the 1920s was say "Well, I haven't really thought about it too much."

On Blame

At the very best, no human being can hope to anticipate more than a few of the more commonplace situations which the quarter will have to face. And the minor variations in even those may vitally alter the wisdom of any set policy. The quarter-back who has been systematically discouraged in the use of his own judgment certainly cannot be fairly blamed when in some unforeseen emergency he looks blankly over to the side-lines and grabs desperately for some preconceived play designed to fit the circumstances.

William W. Roper, *Winning Football*, 1921

You hear that? That means every time you goofed on one of the Mannings doing a face, *you* were the jerk. Them boys can't help it!

On Timing

Another very serious charge against football as sport lies in the mere chance of time that closes the first half, and remands the game to a practically new beginning with the beginning of the second half. Harvard may be upon the point of scoring, a touch-down is not merely in sight but almost within grasp, but the minute arrives and time is called, and all the splendid play counts for naught in the result of the game. . . . [A]nd then Yale fights through the second half with equal skill, only, perhaps, to lose it all within a foot of the goal because another fateful minute has arrived. If we could be sure of such an equality in the game as we have imagined, it might be said that the chance is the same for each side. But, even then, the objection would lie that in neither half would justice be done—it would be only two cases of injustice.

George E. Merrill, *Is Football Good Sport?*, 1903

I can't tell if this is an argument against football or against clocks, but either way the solution is the same: We must play football forever, until the sun burns out and our bodies turn to dust. It's only fair.

On Punting Regimens

Regardless of how much interest a player shows, punting becomes monotonous if taken in too large a dose. So, after the punter has mastered things within the twenty-yard line, he may begin to try his hand, or his foot, at place kicking. It is a welcome change from straight punting.

Walter Camp, *Football Without a Coach*, 1920

Seventy-five years before the debut of Sony's PlayStation, young men were so desperately bored, they were begging to punt. Tragic.

On Children's Games

Again, the ancient life of pursuit and capture persists upon every playground in the familiar games of tag, blackman, pull-away, and a hundred others. Indeed, for the exhibition of this instinct, no organized game is necessary. Sudden playful pursuit and flight are seen wherever children are assembled. The ancient life of personal combat is mirrored in the plays of children in mimic fighting and wrestling. The passion of every boy for the bow and arrow, sling, sling-shot, gun, or anything that will shoot, is merely the persistence of deep-rooted race habits formed during ages of subsistence by these means.

Professor G.T.W. Patrick,
The Psychology of Football, 1913

What are the odds that the game of "blackman" wasn't racist as all hell? I'm going to peg them at approximately ten hundred thousand billion million to one. Might be too low.

The Worst Team Names of All Time

- **Colorado School of Mines**—The Orediggers' mascot is a donkey, which is not so bad in itself. According to the school, however, the real donkey, aka Blaster the Burro, was removed from campus for being too grumpy.
- **Rollins College**—Rollins says they're the only school in the country that dubs its athletes "Tars," which is extremely believable.
- **Tarleton State**—Texans for the men? Fine. TexAnns for the women? Indefensible.
- **Texas A&M-Kingsville Javelinas**— "Javelina" is another name for the peccary, a type of small pig. Pigs are wonderful. Unfortunately, Kingsville's costumed mascots are named Porky and Baby, which is completely unacceptable in every way.
- **Washburn University**—The Ichabods are named for Ichabod Washburn, a guy who made a bunch of wire in the 1800s. He was a dork.
- **University of Central Oklahoma**—Are you really gonna stick with "Bronchos"? Just admit you made a typo and move on, you're not foolin' anybody.
- **Southern New Hampshire University**—Their motto is "The Greatest and the Best," and their mascot is Petey Penmen. These facts should be mutually exclusive.
- **Franklin & Marshall College**—In years to come, "Diplomats" may evolve into a complimentary masculine nickname on par with "Warriors" or "Athletics," but for now it is some major nerd shit for sure.
- **Regis College**—Regis Pride sounds less like a team name and more like a morning show fan club.

- **Rose-Hulman Institute of Technology**—The Fightin' Engineers' logo is a guy punching a spreadsheet. Just kidding. I don't know, though, it might be.
- **Williams College**—Allegedly, the Ephs are named for Ephraim Williams, the founder of the college. But unless he was a purple cow, which is what their mascot is, the name is perplexing as hell. Actually, even if he was a purple cow, the name is bad.
- **Rowan University**—"Whoo RU" the owl represents the Rowan Profs in something like sixteen varsity sports. Decide whether the nickname or the mascot is worse and you win free admission.
- **Whittier College**—Whittier boasts among its alumni former President Richard Nixon, who was so incredibly off-putting that he lost the 1960 election to a young, unknown Catholic—an unthinkable failure for the time. Anyway, Whittier's teams are "The Poets."
- **Simon Fraser University**—Despite being an NCAA Division II school, Simon Fraser is located in British Columbia. So you can kind of forgive them for not knowing that you should never name your team "The Clan," but kind of not. (They even rebranded from "Clansmen" at some point. Come on!)
- **Delta State**—"Statesmen" would suffer from the same sort of wimpiness that plagues "Diplomats" and "Poets" if it weren't juxtaposed with its totally insipid "Lady Statesmen" counterpart. Who is that for, really?
- **Sonoma State**—"Seawolf," huh? Hell, why not? Surely there are worse fictional creatures after which you could be named.
- **Webster University**—Making a portmanteau from the names of two nearby streets is normally a nickname home run, but in this one rare case, "Gorlok" is hopelessly lame.

On Integrity

Officials are generally more efficient and fearless and their rulings are more and more being accepted without quibbling. There are, however, still many school teams, and even some college teams, that seem to fail to recognize that the first obligation of every foot ball player is to protect the game itself, its reputation, and its good name. He owes this to the game, its friends, and its traditions. There can be little excuse for any college player who allows the game to be smirched with unsportsmanlike tactics.

John R. Richards, *Inside Dope on Football Coaching*, 1917

Football Player Responsibilities:

1. No Smirching.
2. Don't shatter your fibula trying to tackle a guy you'd actually like in any other circumstance.
3. Did you smirch?

On Snap Technique

In receiving the ball, the quarterback has, with his hands and arms and body, what may be called three cups. These cups are formed: first, by the hands; second, by the forearms; and third, by the arms and the body. The ball, when tossed by the center to the quarterback, will pass from the ground to the ground in a small arc. The long axis of the ball is always horizontal. The top of this arc is the point at which the ball is received by the hands of the quarterback. At this point the ball has neither an upward nor a downward motion. If the quarterback receives the ball before it reaches the top of its arc, the upward motion of the ball strikes the hands, producing what is known as fighting the ball—that is the ball rebounds from the hands. . . . It is one of the common causes of fumbles.

CHARLES D. DALY, *AMERICAN FOOTBALL*, 1921

The existence of a fourth cup is foretold in the ancient cup scrolls. It is said that there is one who will bear the fourth cup, and that he will change the game forever. He is ultimately destined to be undone by the fifth cup.

COACH TOM SHEA CAPTAIN HARDY

ON PHYSICALITY

Almost equally to be deprecated is the waste of time often devoted to making half-backs of slow heavy weights. Only a quick man can perform a half-back's duties successfully. . . . All this regarding the weight of half-backs applies not only to 'varsity teams, but school teams as well, if one will make the proper proportional changes in weight. That is, a 'varsity player will be called upon to face a forward line averaging one hundred and seventy-five or thereabouts, and men of less than one hundred and thirty-five to one hundred and forty are too light to meet that weight. In school teams the rush line will be some twenty pounds lighter, and the halves can therefore be selected from even one-hundred-and-twenty-five-pound men, if well built.

WALTER CAMP, *AMERICAN FOOTBALL*, 1891

It's more than a little bit sobering to realize that if you're an average guy with a beer belly, you'd be a good thirty pounds heavier than the biggest man to roam 1890s America. It's what being an American in Japan must be like.

On Similarities

The mere act of kicking a football is a good exercise in itself, but very few who do so, particularly among boys, know anything about the game.

In England and her colonies there are innumerable football clubs in every town and village, but in this country the game is largely confined to colleges, and even in these not all the students play. . . . Yet, as it is, when properly played, one of our best out-door games, I think it well that my boy readers should know something about it.

At one time there were fifteen players on a side; now eleven is the legal number. The ground has much the same appearance of a gridiron, and the name "gridiron" is often applied to it, just as "diamond" is applied to the space marked off for that game.

Alfred Rochefort, *Healthful Sports for Boys*, 1910

Until the advent of iPad shuffleboard in the early 2010s, the sport of diamond ball was universally acknowledged as the most expensive and wasteful game in history.

On Scouting

The scout who is to observe a given team during a season makes himself known to the authorities upon his arrival in town, and the game begins. He becomes the guest of the team which it is his duty to observe. Not infrequently he actually dines at the rival training-table and is on perfectly harmonious terms with the rival coaches. On his side, he expects and desires to see and hear nothing except what takes place on the field and is open to the observation of every spectator.

Percy H. Haughton, *Football, and How to Watch It*, 1922

Sometimes the scout will even show up at a rival coach's home and say hello personally. Of course, he'll have the customary dinner and dessert, perhaps with brandy or port. It would be odd, after all this, if the scout didn't offer to clean up afterward. And if he sleeps with somebody's wife, well, it's just good sportsmanship, is all.

On Usefulness

[Harvard kicker Charles] Brickley himself is a fine sample of football genius, although his kicking is so spectacular as to rob him of credit due for other good points of play. He is the popular type of football hero, but would be a great asset to any team even if he could not kick at all.

Herbert Reed, *Football for Public and Player*, 1913

He's the only guy who can afford a football. They're like a million dollars at this point in history. You gotta kill a whole horse to get one. He plays by himself.

On Feet

It will be noticed that in nearly every case the same play can be executed upon the other side of the centre. The choice of sides is purely arbitrary, and had better be decided according to the ability of the runner to execute the movement to best advantage. Some runners prefer to dodge upon the right foot, while others will prefer the left foot.

Walter Camp and Lorin F. Deland, *Football*, 1896

Certain other runners have begun to employ an experimental "two-footed" approach. This method tends to increase speed, balance, and elusiveness, but it all comes at the expense of hilarious hopping.

ON MILKING

Another poetic allusion, from the pen of Sir Thomas Wotton, and which is quoted approvingly by Isaak Walton in the "Compleat Angler," presents a characteristic of the football man which has survived to the present day:

Joan takes her neat rubb'd pail and now
She trips to milk the sand red cow,
Where for some sturdy football swain
Joan stirs a syllabub or twain

PARKE H. DAVIS, *FOOTBALL: THE AMERICAN INTERCOLLEGIATE GAME*, 1917

That feeling when your poetic allusion is quoted approvingly in the "Compleat Angler."

On Playbooks

It is funny to watch the pride with which some coaches invent signal systems which really need a code-book and an index to be interpreted. I remember one particular instance in which a coach had devoted tremendous effort to evolving a system elastic enough to accommodate itself to a repertory of a hundred and sixty-three actual plays! Without even referring the wisdom of providing a quarter of that repertory, the mere cumbersome complexity of the signal system leads up to a story.

William W. Roper, *Winning Football*, 1921

One hundred and sixty-three plays?! My God, how many do you really need? There's throwing it, running it, kicking it . . . what else? Passing it? That's the same thing as throwing it, though. Any more than three plays and you're wasting ink.

On Interceptions

The danger of interception, though much over rated by many, should be carefully guarded. The interception of a long pass often means nothing worse than punting to the other team would have meant. Possession of the ball does not count for as much as in the old game. It should never mean worse if the danger of interception is properly guarded. Too often, however, it means a touchdown for the defense.

Elmer Berry, *The Forward Pass in Football*, 1921

"Interceptions aren't so bad," of course, being the less-popular corollary to the "Score or not, who cares?" maxim of the "Winning is pointless" school of thought.

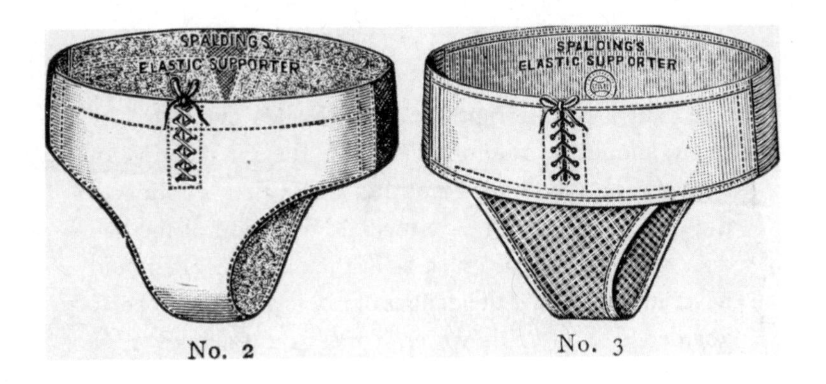

No. 2 No. 3

On Guard Glamour

The position of guard on a football team is usually regarded as prosaic and unattractive. That's partly because a guard never runs with the ball and partly because he is usually instructed to remain in defensive position to stop assaults aimed directly at his location. This last means that he is merely the under dog in a badly messed-up situation, for attacks at guards are usually of a mass nature and do not often offer him opportunities for clean and brilliant-looking tackles such as centers or ends or halves can make in the open field.

John W. Heisman, *Principles of Football*, 1922

Telling a guard he's not as fancy as a center is like telling a urinal it's not as useful as a toilet. Sure, it's true enough, but man, it hurts to hear.

ON BATHING

In the first place, one bath a day is enough, and any other should be a mere sponging and rubbing. Men who indulge in a tub in the morning and then spend another fifteen minutes in a plunge after practice in the afternoon get too much of it. Again, the habit of spending a long time under the shower every day is a mistake. It feels so refreshing after a hard practice that a man is tempted to stay too long, and it does him no good. The best and safest plan is to take a light, quick sponge bath in the morning immediately upon rising, and then, after practice in the afternoon, to take just a moment under the shower, and follow it by a good rubbing.

WALTER CAMP, *AMERICAN FOOTBALL*, 1891

"Careful not to bathe too much" and other nuggets from the time of cholera and outdoor toilets.

On Mentoring

Despite the principle of supply and demand, there may be reasons why the athletic coach should not receive three times as much salary as the professor of Greek; but there is no inherent reason why he should not hold a position of equal dignity. He can do more good than the professor of Greek, and a great deal more harm. Thus faculty control in athletics should be like faculty control in Greek or economics or chemistry—not intervention in details, but that power of adjustment in common interests which may fitly be exercised over a department of physical education. . . . There is no more reason why the teacher of football should curse his pupils than why the teacher of Greek should curse his, who may be quite as exasperating; and there is every reason why the leader whose manners and conduct are more catching than any other's should lead straight, whether on or off the field.

Raymond Gettel, "*The Value of Football*," 1922

Yeah, I guess mistranslating a line from *The Iliad* is equally as annoying as launching your body with tremendous force at the wrong person, place, or time with millions of dollars at stake. Or it's at least close, anyway.

The Most Dominant Teams Before Elvis Roamed The Earth

- **1950–55 Cleveland Browns (58-13-1)**
  The Browns arguably got better from here—though their playoff record wouldn't necessarily show it—by adding MVP and HOFer Jim Brown to a stacked title team. But Elvis really took off around 1956, and that is the arbitrary standard I assigned to myself when I was developing this book months ago, so we are cutting them off at 1955. It's just as well, since that year was their penultimate championship, and serves as one of the final reminders of the franchise's non-futility.

- **1945 Army Cadets (9-0)**
  This hard-nosed team of roustabouts kicked the ever-living hell out of stalwarts like Navy, Notre Dame, Penn, Michigan, Duke, and also Hitler. An excellent vintage.

- **1954–56 Oklahoma Sooners (31-0)**
  The Sooners ran roughshod over the other six teams (assuming conference names were at that point still accurate) in the Big Seven under the tutelage of Hall of Fame coach Bud Wilkinson, stacking up a gaudy record and a handful of national titles. In 1956, Oklahoma's stifling defense would shut out six of its ten opponents and stay in the number-1 slot from the season's start to finish.

- **1972 Miami Dolphins (17-0)**
  There's some evidence to suggest that the Dolphins were a good deal luckier than they were good, but they did go 17-0 and that's that. But if you ask me, they could have gone 1700-0 and I'd still get annoyed hearing about the champagne popping parties every year when the last undefeated team loses a game.

- **1922–23 Canton Bulldogs (21-0-3)**
  The only games they have in Canton now are the Hall of Fame games, which take place in the preseason and are consistently terrible. Unless they canceled it, which they may very well have, and should have if they didn't. It's really quite striking how virtually everything the NFL does outside the core regular and postseason games is such useless garbage, isn't it? Anyhow, interestingly enough, despite the three ties, the Bulldogs were actually considered to have had a perfect winning percentage, since nobody really gave a damn back then and that's just the way it was.
- **1953 Maryland Terrapins (10-1)**
  The Terps! Who knew, right? So they lost once, but it hardly seems fair to dock these guys for going down to the 1954 Sooners—who totally whipped ass by the way—by the tally of 0-7 in the Orange Bowl. That's a damn fine showing, especially considering Maryland handled Ole Miss and Alabama, both then-ranked number 11, in consecutive weeks by a combined score of 59-0.
- **1942 Chicago Bears (11-1)**
  It's a similar story for the 1942 Bears, though magnified a bit by their two consecutive championships coming into the season and the departure of Head Coach George Halas in November of 1942 to fight in World War II. They did lose to the Redskins, though, so never mind. They stunk.
- **1930 Notre Dame Fighting Irish (10-0)**
  The Irish would have to share the championship spoils with Alabama, which I'm sure was no less lame then than it was in 2003. Coach Knute Rockne would famously go on to crash his plane in disappointment over the split title. Just kidding. His plane did crash, though.

On The Layout

The football field is not hard to mark out; as in baseball, the flatter and smoother the better. The field is rectangular, one hundred and sixty feet wide by three hundred and thirty feet long. For convenience in telling the position of the ball, lines, indicated by whitewash as in tennis, are drawn across the field, fifteen feet apart.

In laying out, measure eighty feet from one corner along the line and mark the point. On the opposite end mark in the same way. The end lines being one hundred and sixty feet long, the points indicated will mark the center of the lines. Next measure nine feet three inches to the right. . . .

Alfred Rochefort, *Healthful Sports for Boys*, 1910

Building a proper football field is simple enough for most handy men, and can be done in a week's end if all supplies are in order. All told, out-of-pocket expenditures should come in well south of $1 billion worth of hotel taxes. Perhaps no more than half that, if the timber market is agreeable.

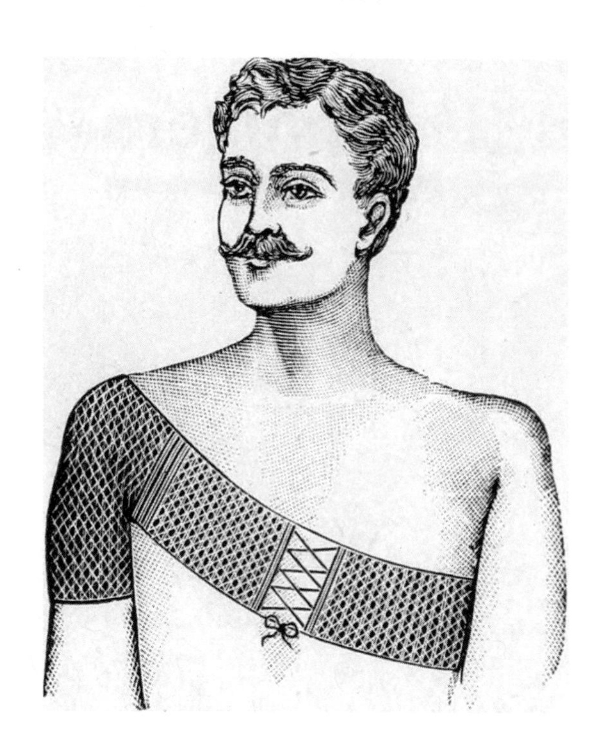

On Impulses

On the other hand, it must be understood that extreme fatigue often greatly increases the strength of sex impulses, and at the same time weakens the resisting power. The uneliminated waste products in the system and the general depression of fatigue lowers moral resistance. The football player's periods of greatest temptation, for example, are likely to follow the big game.

M. J. Exner, MD, *The Rational Sex Life for Men*, 1914

This theory pretty neatly explains why all those people freeze to death humping at the top of Mount Everest. Well, that, and bored Sherpa dares.

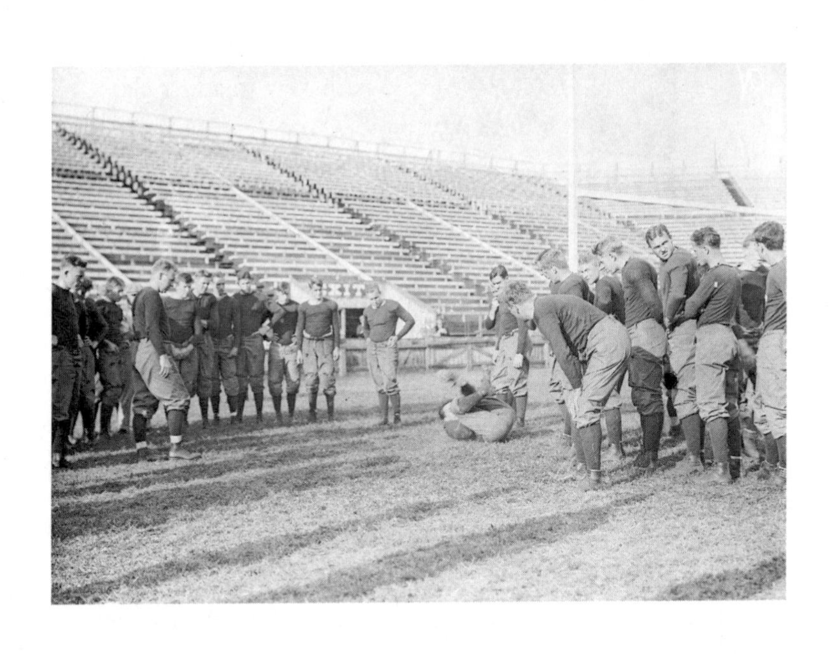

On Order

Never let players squabble or quarrel or fight even in practice scrimmages. Tell them to save all that for the enemy. It is best not even to permit them to indulge in useless talking. Instead, they should keep silent and listen to the coaching, and that way the coach will be able to make his instructions heard without the need of exasperating repetition.

There should be as good order and as business-like an air about all football practice as there is in a first class bank or on a military drill ground.

John W. Heisman, *Principles of Football*, 1922

Football is the perfect combination of banking and the armed forces. Think about it. The sport is full of guys who couldn't succeed anywhere else, whose consciences are whittled down to nothing in the pursuit of a goal they can't possibly understand or benefit from, and who ultimately become public liabilities once their private overlords decide they've become too much of a burden. And on the other side of it, football is like the military because they both have uniforms.

On Puns

At Williams one afternoon, Fred Daly, former Yale Captain and coach at Williams, in trying forward passes instructed his ends to catch them at every angle and height. One man continually fumbled his attempt, just as he thought he had it sure. He was a new man to Daly, and the latter called out to him:

"What is your name?" Back came the reply, which almost broke up the football practice for the day: "Ketchum is my name."

William H. Edwards, *Football Days: Memories of the Game and of the Men behind the Ball*, 1916

Teammates Charles Dewey and Philbert Howe seemed for some reason to be especially pleased by the revelation.

On Resistance

The early successes of the forward pass were secured almost solely upon the principle of putting the passer a distance of fifteen yards back, then letting the opposing line come charging through absolutely without resistance. Practically the whole offensive team was sent down to receive (apparently) the pass, thus confusing the defense as to who was eligible and furnishing interference as soon as the pass was completed. By actual experiment it was found that a distance of thirteen to fifteen yards was necessary. Although lines are more wary and experienced today than formerly, this single piece of strategy is still very valuable. Many teams are failing with their passes simply because their passer is not more than seven to ten yards back.

Elmer Berry, *The Forward Pass in Football*, 1921

You know, if you really want to keep your passer safe, even fifteen yards back might not be enough. Why not put him someplace the opposing team can't possibly go, say, in your locker room? That'll leave 'em scratchin' their heads!

On Field Conditions

Quarterbacks should watch carefully the condition of the field and take any possible advantage of any conditions that may prevail. On a sloppy field, a quarterback will keep his eyes open for a dry spot, and when he finds it he will use it for staging a run. On a field that slopes downhill toward a side line, a wise quarter, needing a certain distance, may elect to try this downhill run rather than to buck away up toward the middle.

Walter Camp, *Football Without a Coach*, 1920

Rarest Things of the 1920s:
Swimsuits without stripes
Rhino Horn
Dry, level fields
Shooting stars

On Antiquaries

Antiquaries at Harvard claim that a football was kicked promiscuously about the Yard in a simple game as early as 1800. A few years later some genius devised a contest between the Freshmen and Sophomores. To-day it would be called a rush instead of a game but since it possessed a few crude rules of order and was played with a football it must be accredited as the lineal progenitor of the fully perfected organism that to-day is presented upon Soldiers Field.

Parke H. Davis, *Football: The American Intercollegiate Game*, 1917

"Hey, let's pair off. Could be fun."
—The Football Genius

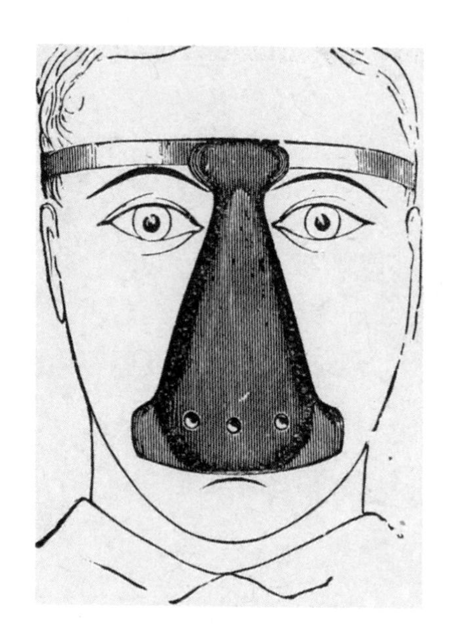

On Stupidity

I find emphatically, that it does not pay to go too far in trying to devise a system which cannot be decoded by the enemy. It is better to run a fair risk of having the signals solved during the game than to face the certainty that every one of them will mean a mental effort for one's own eleven and that a goodly share of them will lead to confusion. For that matter the so-called addition system practically defies detection except on long and close study, even though every opponent knows that it is being used.

William W. Roper, *Winning Football*, 1921

Football was born in the fiery crucible of the Ivies, and even in that time and place, its adherents were widely considered so inconveniently stupid that they could hardly be trusted to know what they were doing half the time. Makes you feel pretty good about losing the remote all the time, though, right?

On Analogies

A remarkable similarity exists between war and football. This is particularly manifest in their organization. In both war and football we have the staff and the troops. In both, we have the supply department, medical branch, and the instruction branch. In both the importance of leadership is paramount. The principles of war laid down by Clausevitz are the principles of the application of force. Just so in football, we have exactly analogous principles of the application of force and a similar organization.

Charles D. Daly, *American Football*, 1921

In both, we force the rookies to dig a large hole several hundred yards away from home base expressly for pooping.

On Hours

The football season proper is a race against time. Its duration is approximately ten weeks, but allowing for seven or eight games there remains only time enough for some fifty practice sessions, which average not over two hours daily. It follows that the total time allowed a coach to carry out his program of preparation is roughly one hundred hours.

Percy H. Haughton, *Football, and How to Watch It*, 1922

If a coach only has approximately 100 hours for instruction per season, and full mastery of the game would require 10,000 hours, it stands to reason that coaches improve at a rate of 1 percent year over year. Therefore, any football coach is very likely to approach 100 years of age before achieving competency. QED.

On Stillness

It is in the course of the final games of the season that the duty of the coach becomes most arduous. Prohibited by the rules from directing the team from the side lines, he must stand still with tense muscles and note every movement and every play of his men which will carry the team through to victory or defeat. The policy he has laid out may be reversed, and yet he would be powerless to order any change. Between the halves, however, the half that is past may be gone over and the half to come discussed, and measures taken to correct the errors and weaknesses developed by the early part of the game.

W. Cameron Forbes, "The Football Coach's Relation to the Players," *Outing Volume 37*, 1901

Penalty, home team, coach movement! The coach was not still during play. Penalty, away team, coach not tense! The coach was visibly relaxed. By rule, those fouls offset. Repeat first down.

On Blowouts

Another and, so far as this paper will allow, a final objection to football as sport is the great inequality in the scores that almost always is to be marked through any season. Given a list of games between colleges, small or large, a great majority of the scores will show such inequalities as 21 to 0; 56 to 0; 45 to 6, etc. With great rarity ties are recorded, and of hardly less exceptional record are the games that show any approach to equal skill and strength.

George E. Merrill, *Is Football Good Sport?*, 1903

Blowouts are no fun to watch; this sport needs more ties!

ON STRENGTH IN NUMBERS

Football, sometimes called a game of war, differs from war in this respect, that it is not possible to win over an enemy by superiority of numbers, for each team can have only eleven men. The strength of the eleven depends upon the superiority of the individuals, and the superior skill in fighting these eleven best men against the best eleven of some other college or university.

WILLIAM H. LEWIS, "MAKING A FOOTBALL TEAM,"
OUTING VOLUME XLI, 1903

Depending on which Svengali you asked, in the early twentieth century, football was either exactly like war or *almost* exactly like war, at least as the latter was understood to have existed at that time. Now that actual war involves drones, however, the comparisons of heaving a lateral to running a teenager through with a bayonet mostly seem to have abated.

On Dismemberment

It is not to be intimated, or understood, that any coach would be so self-seeking, or any school expect so much, that any man should be called upon to sacrifice the equivalent of a limb. It is not to be presumed that a coach would be so brutal as to take any unnecessary chances with his men. But it is entirely reasonable to require that men of the calibre desired for a football team be willing to make such a sacrifice.

Maj. Frank W. Cavanaugh, *Inside Football*, 1919

Counterpoint: It is actually not reasonable to do that, at all.

On Slumps

Not infrequently there comes a time in the course of the team's development when the entire squad is in what is known as a "slump." This is usually at about mid-season, and just after the first really hard game against a high-class opponent. If the team has played poorly in the game the coaches will be hungry to get at the men and anxious to lay out the hardest kind of daily work. It is a natural temptation, for the coaches themselves probably will be under fire by the undergraduate body and the alumni. . . .

The "slump" is really apt to be due to the fact that the men are "overfootballed" just as a man may be "over-golfed."

Herbert Reed, *Football For Public and Player*, 1913

Over-golfed, adj. [oh-ver-gawl-fid]

1. A condition resulting from having played too much golf or consumed too much beer while golfing
2. Golf-sickness, i.e. Golfed-out
3. Fat

On Compromise

> The first steps towards a joint football organization were taken in 1863, when a number of the London Rugby clubs attempted to draw up a uniform code of laws which should be acceptable to all parties. In the mean time, the more enthusiastic followers of the dribbling game had come to an agreement over their rules, and formed themselves into the "Football Association." A joint conference was next held between the Rugbeians and the Dribblers for the purpose of effecting a compromise upon the points in which the two games differed.
>
> Walter Camp and Lorin F. Deland, *Football*, 1896

The Great Dribbler Massacre of 1863, as it came to be known, was among the bloodiest and most influential conflicts in Football War history. Few Dribblers survived, and those who did and were able to evade capture went totally underground. Decades later, the leaders of the Rugbeians were tried at The Hague and summarily executed for crimes against humanity, but their indelible mark on the history of kicking a ball around in the yard remains.

On Individuality

A team with poor ends is in a bad way. The ends are of vast importance and the position calls for speed, versatility and exceptional ability in tackling. This tackling must be the deadly sort and the kind that invariably holds the runner. There is more room for individuality in end play than in most line positions, but certain things must be done by an end and no individual idea or style can be allowed to interfere with their performance.

John R. Richards, *Inside Dope on Football Coaching*, 1917

It's cool how even a hundred years before $10,000 fines for wearing the wrong color socks, football at the professional level has begun to sound like a terrible spinoff of *The Giver*. You gotta respect how much effort these guys put into making sure no one had fun with the game ever.

On Hooligans

Sunday morning these fine fall days are taken up with reading about the "40,000 football enthusiasts" or the "gaily-bedecked crowd of 60,000 that watched the game on Saturday." And so they probably did, unless there were enough men in big fur coats who jumped up at every play and yelled "Now we're off!" thus obstructing the view of an appreciable percentage.

Robert Benchley, *Of All Things*, 1921

The concept of a disruptive jerk in 1921 was a mildly excited rich guy. If he showed up to a Buffalo Bills game today, he'd get put through a folding table before the game even started.

On Switching Gears

> No matter what method of signalling be used, there is one important feature to be regarded, and that is, some means of altering the play after a signal has been given. This is, of course, a very simple thing, and the usual plan is to have some word which means that the signal already given is to be considered void, and a new signal will be given in its place. . . . It is very unwise not to be prepared for such an emergency, because if a captain is obliged to have time called and personally advise his team one by one of such a change, the opponents are quite sure to see it and to gain confidence from the fact that they have been clever enough to make such a move necessary.
>
> Walter Camp, *American Football*, 1891

All right, men! Everyone line up, single file! It has come to my attention that the time to devise a new play is upon us! I shall come at you in order, from left to right, and hand each player a slip of paper onto which three choices for a new play have been scrawled. We will draw straws for foreman, and hear arguments as to each selection, breaking once for lunch, and reconvening to select a new direction for our side. Please hold all questions until . . . Fitzgerald, back to your huddle, old sport!

On Common Knowledge

A number of writers have given detailed and fairly clear instructions as to how a forward pass may or should be thrown, but I do think there is need for this here: all boys, even in the grammar grades, are fairly familiar with the basic principles involved.

John W. Heisman, *Principles of Football*, 1922

Yeah, I think probably most people understand how to throw something. A lot of animals do too, I think. Elephants can wing a branch or whatever pretty far, and those guys don't even have hands.

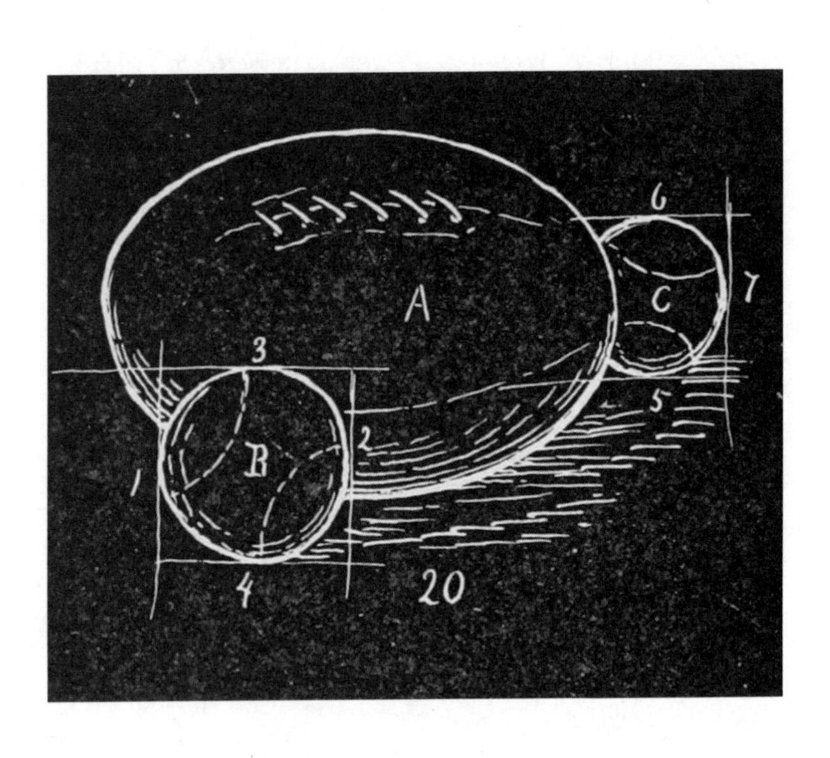

A
B
C
1
2
3
4
5
6
7
20

On Heels

When a kicked ball is caught on the fly by one of the opposite side, the catcher marks with his heel on the ground the spot where the catch was made. The catcher then shouts, "Fair Catch," or he may hold up one hand.

Beyond the heel mark the opponents of the catcher cannot advance till the ball is again put in play. The catcher is entitled to the privilege of falling back towards his own goal, as far as he chooses; from the point selected he may take a place-kick, a drop-kick, or a punt. Instead of this, he may choose to give the ball to one of his own side for a "scrimmage." . . .

Any player on this side may now take out the ball; he makes a mark as he walks by twisting his heel. When he has reached a point that suits, he places the ball for one of his own side to kick.

Alfred Rochefort, *Healthful Sports for Boys*, 1910

It's striking how much of the game depended on heels back in the day. If you wanted to play football but didn't have good heels, you were pretty much screwed.

On Sucky Gifts

I value more highly than any other athletic gift I have ever received, the Princeton football championship banner that hangs on my wall. It was given to me by a friend who sent three boys to Princeton. It is a duplicate of the one that hangs in the trophy room of the gymnasium there.

William H. Edwards, *Football Days: Memories of the Game and of the Men behind the Ball*, 1916

Kudos to this guy for very subtly saying all the other athletic gifts he ever got were super crummy. "Ah, my favorite banner. It's not even the real one, just a copy, but is so much better than my other presents. How I love it, and hate the other ones."

On Bad Nicknames

Now for a word about passing the ball from one to another. The ball assumes a natural position when properly held. If a player learns to hold the ball properly he will never be known as a fumbler, and "fumbler" is the worst name that can be applied to anybody on a good team.

Walter Camp, *Football Without a Coach*, 1920

Really? How about "Jerry the Drunken Pedophile"? I think I'll take "fumbler," thanks.

SCRIBNER'S

FOR NOVEMBER
The Game by Wire
A
Football Story
THE PATH TO
JAMESTOWN
BY
SIDNEY LEE
NOW ON SALE
TWENTY-FIVE
CENTS

On Attacks

> The actual catching of the pass is not essentially different from catching a punt or any ordinary pass. One hand should be used to guide the ball into the body, one hand should be kept well under the ball, the elbows should be kept close and the ball always be brought in *against the body* and held securely against any possible attack.
>
> Elmer Berry, *The Forward Pass in Football*, 1921

Any possible physical attack, that is. There is no grip that can adequately protect the player from a well-timed verbal strike. If you're never going to live up to your father's legacy, in other words, or if you're a selfish jerk, perhaps, you cannot cradle the football in a way that will make you feel any better. You just have to go to therapy like the rest of us.

On Organic Beginnings

The development by these schools of football, from a mere sport without rules or organization, into a highly specialized game was wholly inartificial. At no time during its formative period was an interscholastic convention or even a conference held between two schools. The idea of an interscholastic contest did not occur until years after the perfection of the game. This unexpected circumstance is due to the fact that each school originated a style of game peculiar to itself and found sufficient entertainment in the struggles of teams organized within its own walls.

Parke H. Davis, *Football: The American Intercollegiate Game*, 1917

An alternate hypothesis: There were no phones or cars, so nobody went anywhere or did anything.

On Misinformation

For myself I prefer to let as many men as possible feel that they are Varsity material and give as few men as possible the idea that they are Varsity certainties.

William W. Roper, *Winning Football*, 1921

"I love lying!"

ON DAYS OF THE WEEK

Organized practice each day rarely can consume more than two and one-half hours. There are ten weeks in the regular football season. Games are played on Saturdays, leaving five days per week for practice—that is, 5 × 10 × 2½ hours, or 125 hours. Therefore, it is true that the preparation of a team for its final contest is a race against time.

CHARLES D. DALY, *AMERICAN FOOTBALL*, 1921

Fun fact: Sundays would not be invented until Spring 1975.

On Decorum

In other words, business, occupation for the good of society, necessary and unavoidable, may justify such risks, but they do not belong to good sport. The "Journal of the American Medical Association" gives the number of deaths from football accidents in the year 1902 as twelve.

George E Merrill, *Is Football Good Sport?*, 1903

Twelve deaths in a single year is disturbing, and the tongue-in-cheek reference to the "Dirty Dozen" seemed outright inappropriate for a medical journal. But Rodney Dangerfield was the editor that year, and he was determined to sell a bundle.

On Punctuality

If it is one of the big final games of the season to which we are going, I trust we have allowed plenty of time on account of the congestion of traffic—the neck of the bottle—which always occurs at the approach to the field, and have arrived at least twenty minutes ahead of the scheduled time of the game.

Percy H. Haughton, *Football, and How to Watch It*, 1922

And don't forget, a weirdly hostile stranger is going to demand to thumb through our large leather billfolds and cigarette cases on the way into the arena, so allow time for that.

On Friendships

It is not only in knowledge of football that a coach may show his value to the team. He must have friendship and sympathy with the men and with his fellow coaches. . . . The coach must know how to bring out and use the combined knowledge of all of the coaches within his reach.

The friendships with the men are an important feature of the work, and without these friendships and sympathy no coach can hope to obtain the best results. The qualities which go to make up the man who fights his way through a large field of competitors to a position on one of our university teams are qualities which command admiration and respect.

W. Cameron Forbes, "The Football Coach's Relation to the Players," *Outing Volume 37*, 1901

The player-coach relationship should resemble those famous friendships, in which one friend is the other friend's boss, and makes a hundred times the cash that the employee friend makes in free meals, T-shirts, and video games.

On Visions

Sir Samuel Pepys records somewhere in his diaries, that on looking out of his window one frosty morning, he found the street covered with footballs. Now that the season of autumn sport has arrived, one will not be surprised to repeat Sir Samuel's experience in passing any athletic field, college campus, or school grounds.

William H. Lewis, "Making a Football Team,"
Outing Volume XLI, 1903

Hey, or maybe you could start picking up after yourself when you play a game? I may not be a knight of the realm, but I can fill a basket full of toys. One at a time.

On Slight Lameness

The wearing of very light clothing is advisable during these early sessions, often undertaken during one of summer's late revivals; and all candidates should be warned to report fatigue or the slightest lameness in arm or leg.

The players may be divided into squads of a dozen, and sent ambling around the field, throwing the ball from one to another; perhaps choosing sides and making a semi-basketball affair out of it, but always with a sharp eye to exhaustion.

Maj. Frank W. Cavanaugh, *Inside Football*, 1919

Ah yes, *A Semi-Basketball Affair*, Will Ferrell's biggest box office flop.

On Pace

A game that inspires such widespread devotion must rest upon certain vital underlying principles of human nature.

A certain amount of its popularity, especially from the spectator's standpoint, may undoubtedly be explained by that fondness for excitement and for spectacular display which, especially in America, seems a logical corollary to the intense and nervous pace of our living. But a closer analysis of the fundamental nature of the game and of the physical, mental, and moral requisites of its players, shows that it reproduces, in unusual fashion, many of the essential features in human development.

Raymond Gettel, "*The Value of Football,*" 1922

And now that Americans are almost certainly the most sedentary and lackadaisical creatures in human history, we still really like football a lot. I guess, if you think about it, that was a dumb opinion after all.

NEXT!

A president who "does" things.

On Term Limits

Another great evil, only hinted at by President Eliot, is the presence of the professional coach, the promoter of public athletics, who makes his living through winning victories and who goes as far in securing them as a relaxed public opinion in town and in university will let him. The self-respect of the colleges demands a declaration of independence in this regard. A rule that should be adopted, if we must have paid coaches, is that each coach must have been student or alumnus in the institution he represents, and that the academic life of a paid coach like that of an athlete shall be limited to four years.

David Starr Jordan, *Football: Battle or Sport*, 1908

Oh, yeah? You think it's wrong that coaches make tons of money with virtually no oversight in a system that exploits young men and endangers their health? Ha! Well, uh, hey are you still alive?

Wow, no, you're not. Not even close. Sorry. Yikes.

On Contrasts

The real health of American football lies in our schools and universities, while the saving grace of English football is to be found in the great clubs, like Blackheath and the Harlequins, and the international fifteens of England, Ireland, Scotland and Wales, combinations that no university team could hope to meet with anything like an equal chance for victory.

Englishmen have the game they want, while we have, in the main, the game we want; the English game is built around a Plan, and woe betide him who takes too many liberties with it, while the American game is a mass of plans and stratagems.

Herbert Reed, *Football For Public and Player*, 1913

You ever notice how Americans play football like *this*, and Englishmen play football like *THIS?* Right? Let's see. What else is in the news. So I just moved into a new apartment . . .

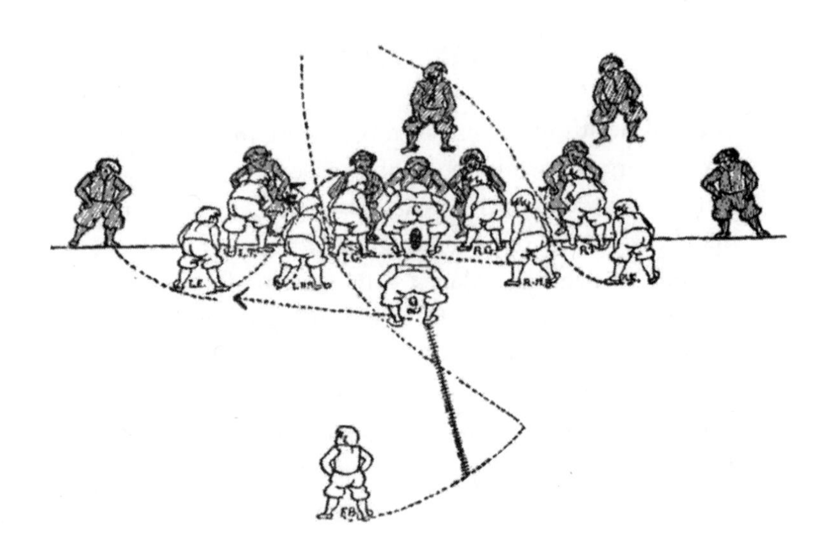

ON LARGE *HOLES*

Play XXVII
Small Wedges Outlet No 2
Ball to full-back. The left hand wedge must make the hole, and left half-back is responsible for this. Let him call on the left end if needed. Right half-back should go inside the quarter and push opposing tackle outwards. If the dodge is well executed and sufficiently pronounced, the runner will find a large hole awaiting him.

WALTER CAMP AND LORIN F. DELAND, *FOOTBALL*, 1896

Sounds pretty good, but how big of a hole are we talking about? (Insert "your mama's so fat" joke here.)

On Subtraction By Subtraction

Elements of Playing Center

> The successful carrying out of the duties devolving upon a center, is so necessary to a team, that it seems that this position like several others, can be classed as the most important on a team. Indeed, we could not play the game minus a center—or minus any of the players, for that matter.
>
> John R. Richards, *Inside Dope on Football Coaching*, 1917

Well, and I guess you couldn't play without the coaches, either. And you'd have to have a field. There wouldn't be much point without fans, either. You'll need a place for them to sit and all and concessions. What else? The ball! Man, this is starting to sound like a big hassle. Let's just forget it.

On Extremely Normal Breakfasts

Seven o'clock is a good time for an athlete in training to rise. He ought to get a good dry-rubbing, and then sponge his body with cold water, or have a shower-bath, with a thorough rubbing afterwards. He will then go out to exercise before breakfast, not to run hard, as is commonly taught, but to walk briskly for an hour, while exercising his lungs in deep-breathing. Before this walk, an egg in a cup of tea, or something of the kind, should be taken.

Walter Camp, *American Football*, 1891

Athletes should definitely stick to the breakfast classics: tea eggs, OJ doughnut dunkers, cigarette salads, that kind of thing.

On Diversification

No offense can be considered well rounded or dependable that cannot show strength in all four departments—end running, line bucking, forward passing and punting. Therefore, do not neglect any of them.

John W. Heisman, *Principles of Football*, 1922

Well, being good in sports is pretty simple. Just pay attention to every aspect of the game and you're good to go.

William H. Dietz, The Football Beau Brummel
…otos …tesy … Goodwin

On Epiphanies

To every man there comes a moment that marks the turning point of his career. For me it was a certain Saturday morning in the autumn of 1891. As I look back upon it, across the years, I feel something of the same thrill that stirred my boyish blood that day and opened a door through which I looked into a new world.

William H. Edwards, *Football Days: Memories of the Game and of the Men behind the Ball*, 1916

I found a box of girlie magazines in the woods.

On Humorists

"Whin I was a young man," said Mr. Dooley, "an' that was a long time ago,—but not so long ago as manny iv me inimies'd like to believe, if I had anny inimies,—I played fut-ball, but 'twas not th' fut-ball I see whin th' Brothers' school an' th' Saint Aloysius Tigers played las' week on th' pee-raries.

"Whin I was a la-ad, iv a Sundah afthernoon we'd get out in th' field where th' oats'd been cut away, an' we'd choose up sides. Wan cap'n'd pick one man, an' th' other another. 'I choose Dooley,' 'I choose O'Connor,' 'I choose Dimpsey,' 'I choose Riordan,' an' so on till there was twinty-five or thirty on a side. Thin wan cap'n'd kick th' ball, an' all our side'd r-run at it an' kick it back; an' thin wan iv th' other side'd kick it to us, an' afther awhile th' game'd get so timpischous that all th' la-ads iv both sides'd be in wan pile, kickin' away at wan or th' other . . . .

"Mr. Dooley on the Game of Football" by Finley Peter Dunne, an excerpt from *The Wit and Humor of America* edited by Marshall P. Wilder, 1911

I have no idea what this says. I think it's supposed to be a funny story. It cost a lot of money to print this page because of all the apostrophes, though.

Descriptions Of Twentieth-Century Marching Band Members Looking Miserable in Candid Photographs

- A young man in an all-black suit with prominent buttons glumly holds a clarinet. His right toe is pointed and his large hat is falling over. He looks very unhappy.
- Two men standing next to each other are holding their instruments but not playing them. They look uncomfortable, possibly due to how close they are being forced to stand next to each other. It must be during a break.
- A portly gentleman sweats while blowing into a trumpet. It is clearly wintertime, but he appears sweaty. His cheeks are inflated in an exaggerated fashion.
- Bug's eye perspective shot reveals four to six marchers in full regalia stomping the asphalt. It seems obvious the scene has been composed for the sake of the photo. Instruments may be fake.
- Crestfallen man inexpertly plays trombone. He appears to suddenly realize mid-song that central air conditioning will not be widespread until he is dead.

- A man toots on an alto saxophone. Notice how these are all men? Not one gal. Are you telling me they couldn't find a girl to play the flute or something? Get real.
- A thin man plays a flute. (REALLY?!)
- Bored-looking band director looks out onto field of perfectly arranged marchers in full swing and may well be considering ending his own life.
- Fellow who doesn't totally not resemble a young Dennis Farina appears to enthusiastically slap his bass drum in time with the music. The adjacent percussionists seem annoyed, possibly due to the extremely wide berth his drumsticks seem to require.
- Guy who looks like he was forced to march in the band as punishment for a crime smokes a hand-rolled cigarette far behind the group.
- Boy, tall but otherwise normal-looking, rolls xylophone out onto the outer edges of the track. He is seasonally depressed, but the special lamps that make you feel better have not yet been invented.

On Officiating

Inquisitive Old Gentleman. "Who's won?"

First Football Player. "We've lost!"

Inquisitive Old Gentleman. "What have you got in that bag?"

Second Football Player. "The umpire!"

Mr. Punch's Book of Sport,
edited by J. A. Hammerton, 1910

We're taking him away because he didn't call the game in our favor. We didn't deserve to win, but that didn't stop us from taking our frustrations out on the umpire. He'll never be found again. He was a volunteer, too. And now he'll be among the lost.

On Toiling

The preparation for an important game on the practice field is a grim, joyless performance. The boys, with set, drawn faces, are urged and whipped into line by the coach, whose expression might be likened to that of a groom trying to drive horses from a burning stable. There is little fun or real sport about it, but a dogged and persistent preparation for war.

C. M. Woodward, *Opinions of Educators on the Value and Total Influence of Inter-Collegiate and Inter-Scholastic American Football as Played in 1903–1909*, 1910

Yeah, man, work freaking sucks. No one likes it. I think that was true even in 1910, when the main jobs were picking up horse crap and burning the horse crap for energy.

VOL. LX. No. 1550.
PUCK BUILDING, New York, November 14, 1906.
PRICE TEN CENTS.
"What Fools these Mortals be!"
Puck
LIBRARY of CONGRESS
Two Copies Received
NOV 13 1906
Copyright Entry
COPY B.
Copyright, 1906, by Keppler & Schwarzmann.
Entered at N. Y. P. O. as Second-class Mail Matter.

FRANK A. NANKIVELL

On The Sabbath

Is the playing at football, reding of merry bookes, & such like delectations, a violation or prophanation of the Sabaoth day?

[. . .] Any exercise which withdraweth us from godlines, either upon the Sabaoth, or any other day else, is wicked & to be forbidden. Now who is so grosly blinde, to seeth not, that these aforesaid exercises not only withdraw us from godliness & virtue, but also haile & allure us to wicked|iness and sin: for as concerning football playing: I protest unto you, it may rather be called a friendly kinde of fight, than a play or recreation. A bloody and murdering practise, then a fellowly sporte or pastime.

Phillip Stubbes, *Anatomy of Abuses in England in Shakspere's Youth, A.D. 1583 Part II: The Display of Corruptions Requiring Reformation*, 1583

Am I crazy for thinking this guy would really get into Mixed Martial Arts?

On Horns

The spectator on the stands at the football game in 1911 is going to be more than ever interested in knowing something about the penalties, and what it means when the umpire blows his horn or the referee blows his whistle, and the play stops and the ball is returned to some other place. . . . There are two offenses which are almost never persisted in, but which if held to would result in . . . forfeiture of the game. If such a thing should happen in the early part of the game, it would involve a new complication of returning the money to the spectators. offenses are, first, refusal to obey the referee, and second, deliberate delay of the game after proper warning.

Walter Camp, *Football For The Spectator*, 1911

Every single part of this is wrong. No one cares about the penalties, the game is delayed constantly, and the referees never throw anyone out. Swing and miss on each part of the idea here . . . it's incredible. I will say, though, that I kind of like the idea of giving umpires horns. Hell, give 'em guitars. "Ska Referees: Why Not?"

On Feet

To begin with, a pair of light, durable shoes is the most necessary if one hopes to star. The arrangement of cleats is not vital, although they should be placed well toward the toe of shoe and not allowed to wear off without replacement. Keep the cleats sharp and even. This is very important for it saves the shoe and foot as well. If possible, players should have three pairs of shoes; one pair for practice, one pair for muddy fields, and one pair for the game. The coach. or trainer, should watch his player's feet assiduously.

M. B. Banks, *Modern Foot-ball for Players and Coaches*, 1919

"I'm on it!" —Rex Ryan

On Routine

A Few Simple Rules of Training Must Be Observed:

- Keep the air in your rooms cool and pure.
- Go to bed at 9:45.
- Eat slowly, and rest for a half hour after eating.
- Do not eat fried food, rich pastries, or fresh bread.
- Register your weight before and after playing.

W. H. Lillard, *Football Rudiments*, 1911

A quarter to ten—the ideal bedtime. At 9:30 you feel like you haven't seen enough of *The Daily Show*, and at 10, you've seen way too damn much of it.

On Potent Potables

The American football captain or coach should bear in mind, when reading these various systems, that the use of ale and port seems to be much better borne by those who live in the English climate than upon this side of the water.

Also, that stiff exercise before breakfast has not been proven advantageous to our athletes except as a flesh-reducer, and then only in exceptionally vigorous constitutions.

Also, that tea is not as popular with us as with the men who train in England.

Walter Camp, *American Football*, 1891

This entry is from a book ostensibly introducing football to the American audience. It is written on page 157. How cheap was paper in the 1890s?

On Ancient Origins

In the 22d chapter of Isaiah is found the verse, "He will turn and toss thee like a ball." This allusion, slight as it may be, is sufficient unto the antiquary to indicate that some form of a game with a ball existed as early as 750 years before the Christian era. . . . A more specific allusion of the same period, however, is the passage in the Sixth Book of the Odyssey of Homer familiar, to all schoolboys: "Then having bathed and anointed well with oil they took their midday meal upon the river's banks and anon when satisfied with food they played a game of ball." This game of Nausicaa and her companions, we are told, was not football, but a dance in which the ball was tossed from hand to hand. . . . Another step, however, will bring us to football.

Parke H. Davis, *Football: The American Intercollegiate Game*, 1917

No. Not another step. Let's go back. Let's go back to the dance, please. Thank you.

On Creampuffs

It is better to have too hard than too weak a schedule. The teams played should demand the maximum effort without drawing on the reserve energy. Fifty per cent of them should be such that they could be held in check by the substitutes. However, as intimated, no more insidious element in development can exist than that of a weak schedule.

Charles D. Daly, *American Football*, 1921

Half the teams on your schedule should be so crappy that your starters could have hangovers from hell and you'd still win. The other half should make your squad look like a garbage can full of rainwater. None of these games should be fun. You should all quit. Nothing matters.

Stadium Snacks Of A Bygone Age

- **Animal Crackers**
  With apologies to all the places in the world in which it is customary to eat bugs, animal crackers are among the absolute worst snacks it is possible for fans to consume. For one thing, they're cookies, not crackers, so right off the bat we're in the red. Next, and perhaps most importantly, they taste like nothing. That's bad, because you're supposed to enjoy eating snacks, and as it turns out, it is extremely difficult to enjoy the flavor of thin air.

- **Cigarettes**
  People used to smoke everywhere, all the time, and you will remember that if you are ever fortunate enough to travel to Asia or a place in the middle of the Nevada desert that took a lot of design cues from Asia. Cigarettes were never really ever considered food, but they were included in MREs until 1975, and a few soldiers probably ate 'em when they were bored or if someone dared 'em to.

- **Cracker Jack**
  This mess is still around somehow, which isn't as objectionable as it is befuddling, so I probably can't reasonably include it. But man, is it ever bad. Getting mad just thinking about this sticky garbage. And who's that little man on the front?!

- **10 Cent Beers**
  On the other hand, these bad boys are never coming back, and it's not because of inflation, either. The most infamous Cleveland-area sports gimmick, in 1974, pretty much ruined extremely cheap and practically unlimited alcohol promotions for the rest of us, all because of what I guess could accurately be described as rioting and bedlam.

- **Milk**
  Ordering, paying for, and then drinking an entire glass of cow's milk while sitting in the stands and watching a ball game is just about the saddest damn thing I've ever heard of. I like the ice cream in the little helmet, and I'd take a shake or a malt to the dome, don't get me wrong. But milk?

ILLINOIS FIELD
I
Bristow Adams

On Harvesting Grain

In bringing a scythe around against standing grain you must have noticed that the reaper swings the blade low and with a swift swing that cuts the whole stalk off neatly close to the ground. Were he to attempt to cut off only the tops of the stalks his blade would not meet with the same rooted resistance as it encounters close to the ground, and he would often fail to behead the stalks.

This illustrates why you should go low.

John W. Heisman, *Principles of Football*, 1922

That's right. Also, in this metaphor, the reaper is the defensive coordinator, the field is . . . the field, and the bread is, uhhhh, commercials? Might need a little work. The soil is painkillers maybe?!

FOOT
BALL

ON THE FRENCH PERSPECTIVE

A French writer who paid a visit to England in the seventeenth century describes the game as follows: "En hiver le footbal est un exercice utile et charmant. C'est un ballon de cuir, gros comme la tete et rempli de vent; cela se ballotte avec le pied dans les mes par celui qui le peut attraper; il n'y a point d'autre science." The description given in the last words of this extract is hardly in keeping with the statement that football was "charmant" and "utile." From the fact that it contained very little science and was played solely by the lower classes of the people, it is fair to assume that it was very rough, if not actually brutal. This supposition is further confirmed by the fact that numerous laws were passed, at intervals, imposing a heavy sentence upon any one who played or witnessed a game of football.

WALTER CAMP AND LORIN F. DELAND, *FOOTBALL*, 1896

Furthermore, the picture painted here is hardly one of a "neatular," "respectimous" pursuit, and the idea that this game of football will ever be accepted among the landownerial, gentrifical class is, frankly, humorescent.

In making a forward pass, assume that an opponent is directly in the way and practice rising on your toes and starting the pass from the highest point you can reach. The ball should travel on a line horizontal to the ground.

On Mechanics

In making a forward pass, assume that an opponent is directly in the way and practice rising on your toes and starting the pass from the highest point you can reach. The ball should travel on a line horizontal to the ground.

W. H. Lillard, *Football Rudiments*, 1911

Or, hell, just grip it however you want and throw it wherever. We're still kinda working the kinks out of this thing.

M
J.G. Allen—'05

On Coach Interference

Coaching from the side lines is prohibited in the rules because it is considered an unfair practice. The game is to be played by the players using their own muscle and their own brains. If an onlooker, having seen all the hands in a game of cards, undertook to tell one of the players what card to play, the other players would have just cause to object.

John R. Richards, *Inside Dope on Football Coaching*, 1917

At all times during the game, the head coach must sit upon a horse facing south along the broad side of a swift river. At first whistle, the horse's behind will be clapped, and he shall set off into the distance with his rider in tow. The coach's arms and legs are to be bound with good twine, and his sense muffled by means of cloth and string. He is permitted one eye to guide the horse away from deadly crevasses. The coach is customarily retrieved by boat on the third day after a victory. This is due to fairness and things such as that.

On Timing

I recall many, many occasions in the old days when it had been solemnly agreed between coaches and trainer that a time-limit should be set on the day's practise and when the coaches would overrule the trainer's call of time to put "just five more minutes" on some individual play which they wanted to perfect. These five minutes were nearly always costly, for it is a provable fact that men are hurt far more easily when they are tired than when they are fresh. Time after time these few extra scrimmages cost us the services of somebody we needed badly.

William W. Roper, *Winning Football*, 1921

Sounds like you'd be better off just never having the last five minutes of a practice. Some sports novices may assert that this is a logical paradox, and that in any session of greater than five total minutes, there will always be a final five-minute period, but if they've never sat behind a too-glossy table on a Sunday afternoon deep cable show with a graphics budget that looks like it came from the Pentagon, they can and should be safely ignored.

On Celebration

Every team has a game during the first half of the season when the tackling is ragged. When the players reassemble on the following Monday, I usually indulge in a few remarks concerning individual and collective shortcomings, explaining that they attempted to reach runners with their arms, instead of driving with their shoulders. . . . I then designate a certain day in the near future as "Bloody Wednesday" . . . notifying the squad of the nature of the intended celebration.

A portion of the afternoon in question is used to send unfortunate substitutes down the line with footballs also with full liberty and license to go at any speed possible and to use as much of the field as they may require. The varsity players should make four or five tackles apiece without shirking the test in any respect. The wild man in the open usually proves sufficiently elusive and determined to make the test entirely valid.

Maj. Frank W. Cavanaugh, *Inside Football*, 1919

This method is also a wonderful parenting strategy. Have two kids? One of them misbehaving? Let them hit the other one repeatedly. Problem solved, and you've earned yourself a glass of day wine.

On Friendly Gatherings

When a snap-back is to be made they arrange themselves in this way: Center holds the ball, behind him stands quarterback; more to the rear is full-back, with left half-back and right half-back a little to the front. Flanking these and slightly in advance are the two ends.

Each of these is ready to receive the ball, at a signal from quarter-back. . . .

When the ball is put in play there is a grand rush. The runner with the ball is surrounded by friends who try to force their way through the opposing line.

Alfred Rochefort, *Healthful Sports for Boys*, 1910

And he breaks away! To the 30, to the 40, and he is surrounded by friends just past midfield! Oh my, he was very surrounded by friends on that play. What a thorough surrounding that was there, by his friends. And it looks like we have a flag for excessive friend-surrounding on the play. You hate to see that.

On Mystery

It is the spectator who needs the coaching nowadays, and it is in the hope of clearing away for his benefit and that of the uncoached schoolboy much of the mystery that has been deftly thrown around the game by those in close touch with the great football universities that this book is offered to a sometimes puzzled football public.

Herbert Reed, *Football For Public and Player*, 1913

If you're a fan in this era, you are likely exposed to no more than a dozen or so plays, executed by the same three or four teams, at an excruciatingly slow pace. That could be overwhelming, though, so here's what a bunch of junk coaches think about when they're freezing on the muddy sidelines.

Athletics

On Stretching

First Exercise: (A) Raise arms to horizontal. Move the left foot twelve inches from the right. Slowly bend the fists and lower the arms downward from the elbows. Then curl the fists upward into the armpits bending the head backward meanwhile until you look upward at the ceiling. Take a deep breath as you bend the head back.

(B) Then, without resting, extend the arms straight forward from the shoulders, palms down; let the arms begin to fall and the body to bend forward from the waist, head up, eyes to the front, until the body has reached the limit of motion. . . .

Walter Camp, *Football Without a Coach*, 1920

Second Exercise: Bend at the waist. Grab the left ankle with the right hand, and repeat on the opposite side. Hop forward in an awkward, swirling motion. Howl for five hours. Blow up a balloon. Vigorously grind your teeth.

On Language

I recently saw in print that Professor William James of Harvard had reported, that on one occasion the Harvard coach said to his team as they went on the field to meet Yale, "Now, fellers,—HELL!" This reminds one of what General Sherman said of War, and yet it is several degrees less strong than the language used by one of the coaches in a Missouri-Kansas game last fall, as reported to me.

C. M. Woodward, *Opinions of Educators on the Value and Total Influence of Inter-Collegiate and Inter-Scholastic American Football as Played in 1903-1909*, 1910

Go get the smelling salts, Woodward heard a sailor say "starfish pee" again!

On Intent

Chief among these is that a man may not strike an opponent with his fist, nor may he run into a man who has just kicked the ball, and is thus in a defenseless position, nor may he use his knee or elbow on an opponent, nor intentionally drop on a man who is in a defenseless position on the ground. In other words, actual intentional roughness is strictly forbidden and will be met with penalties.

Walter Camp, *Football For The Spectator*, 1911

The only roughness allowed in football is the unintentional kind . . . you know, like when you run as fast as you can and throw your entire body at a guy's legs when he's looking the other direction. Just accidental stuff like that.

On Concentration

Line men should practice the art of concentration. To fight in a dream is as fatal for them as it is for a pugilist. Eye and mind must be trained to concentration. The underlying principle of eye concentration is that it must be concentrated on the ball. Some coaches will tell their men to watch both ball and opponent. Never was a more fatal error made. The eye cannot watch two fast-moving things at the same time. To tell when the ball moves, the eye must be absolutely concentrated on it.

Charles D. Daly, *American Football*, 1921

In the past it has become fashionable to assert that the successful quarter will be fully capable of—nay, enthusiastic about rubbing his tummy and patting his head, not at different periods throughout the day, but simultaneously. This, as I will explain, is folly of the highest order.

Football's Ugliest Stadiums

Soldier Field (Chicago Bears)
Soldier Field looks like an abandoned government building getting an air conditioning system for a much larger building shoved into it. That is among its more redeeming qualities.

Hard Rock Stadium (Miami Dolphins/Miami Hurricanes)
Hard Rock Stadium has aged about as well as Hard Rock Café and the genre of hard rock, which is to say, it is assuredly on death's door. The arena's sun-bleached interior and dilapidated ceiling tile motif make it look more like a Nickelodeon theme park than a football field.

Everything in Minneapolis
The Metrodome is dead and buried—metaphorically, but also for a time, literally—under a mountain of snow. Replacing it is the more efficient and competently engineered US Bank Stadium, which for all its technical marvel, looks like something a Jawa would drive across Tattoine.

Estes Stadium (Central Arkansas Bears)
The turf is purple and gray. The turf . . . is purple . . . and gray.

Candlestick Park
A windswept Dumpster in the middle of the most expensive city in the country.

Kibbie Dome (Idaho Vandals)
The architecture of the Kibbie Dome is incredibly fascinating. It's a unique, rainbow-style dome structure that's mostly comprised of arched wooden beams. Its goal posts are hung on the wall. The field is below ground. No doubt it is an incredible accomplishment, and stands out among the drab boxes we're used to seeing everywhere. But it's terrible. Sorry.

Johnny "Red" Floyd Stadium (Middle Tennessee State Blue Devils)
It's true enough that people don't go to Murfreesboro, Tennessee, for its architectural splendor, but, good lord, is this ever an awful building. The stark bleachers give the interior all the grandeur of a bloated community college, and the façade would be more at home in a strip mall full of Best Buys. Being within eyeshot of this K'nex-looking thing must be agonizing.

Mercedes-Benz Superdome (New Orleans Saints)
It saved a lot of people's lives. Let's just get that out of the way. During Hurricane Katrina, the Superdome was literally a lifesaver. But, here's the deal: It's a giant toilet. Did you know FEMA paid $115M to have this thing refurbished after it got blown to hell in the storm? Why? And why is it super shiny now? Do they think you can literally polish a turd? Because that's not what it means, man. Not at all.

The Oakland–Alameda County Coliseum
Hey, I think they're doing football here next week, do you want to put some grass where the basepaths are? No? Ok, great. No, I don't give a damn how it looks or plays, I thought you did. Load off my mind.

DING
DING
DING
AMBULANCE
WEEPING-BOOTHS FOR THE TENDER-HEARTED
FOOTBALL
OLAF
EMERIE
HARRISON
CASKIN
COLLAR
BONES
COLLAR
BONES

On Footwear

> Furthermore, no player could deliberately hit the ball with his hand, or throw it forward (i.e., in the direction of his opponents' goal). No hacking or tripping was allowed, nor were players permitted to wear projecting nails, iron plates, or gutta-percha on any part of the boots or shoes. The time of the game was divided into two parts. During the intermission the two teams changed goals, and the kick-off at the opening of the second half was made by the side not having the kick-off at the commencement of the game.
>
> Walter Camp and Lorin F. Deland, *Football*, 1896

It's easy to forget now, but there was a time when the use of gutta-percha was completely and totally verboten in all professional leagues. If it weren't for trailblazers like Terrell Owens (applying some gutta-percha at midfield right on the Cowboys star) and Chad Johnson (most fines in league history for gutta-percha use), gutta-percha might never have experienced the fabulous successes it's having today as a product—nay, a way of life.

PHILIP
LYFORD

On Gaslighting

> Either the coach or the trainer or at least some person in authority in the football department should be a man who will belittle all injuries to the men who receive them; who is always optimistic, while never explanatory; who will talk fight, and enlarge upon the merits of great fighters. But while talking with set purpose in a fixed direction, the trainer, in reality, will work in quite another; and a too rapid loss of weight, when not regained for the most part during the intervals of rest and sleep, is one of the danger signs which put a competent physical director instantly on watch.
>
> Maj. Frank W. Cavanaugh, *Inside Football*, 1919

In addition, there should be at least two individuals tasked with explaining to the players that they are acting crazy right now, and a third person available to request that the player listen to what he sounds like right now. Some of the sport's most successful organizations will also empower an adviser, coach, or other community member to make certain that the player feels trapped and helpless as well.

MENU
Football Dinner.
YORKSHIRE
v.
MAORIS.
Strafford Arms Hotel,
WAKEFIELD,
January 19th, 1889.
England.

On Bean Water

If you are a coffee drinker and feel that breakfast is incomplete without it, drink it, but confine yourself to one cup. Do not take chocolate or cocoa at any time. Milk is good, but if you are short-winded, leave it alone. Water is needed by a man who exercises and you will be thirsty at night; try to eat your dinner with as little water as possible. Drink plenty in the morning and as much during the day as you feel like doing. Do not flood the stomach at your dinner hour. This last suggestion will be the one that calls for will power.

John R. Richards, *Inside Dope on Football Coaching*, 1917

Oh, no, just one cup for me thanks. Between those four ounces of weak brown sludge, the single piece of bacon, a teaspoon of the scooped-out inside of a burned biscuit, and the memory of an egg I smelled, I've got all the energy I need for a full day at work followed by a water-less evening of getting my head punched in by a coalminer named Teddy.

On Nermal Routine

> Good tackling is the result of daily trips to the tackling dummy—Mondays excepted, possibly.
>
> Charles D. Daly, *American Football*, 1921

Mondays are bad days to try the tackling dummy, no doubt about it, but it couldn't hurt to take a tray of lasagna up there and see what happens. If you end up in Abu Dhabi or outside via a perfectly you-shaped hole in the wall, just brush up on the playbook for the day. (Note: To improve odds of a successful drill, do NOT invite a wise-cracking spider or a particularly naïve dog. They will only make matters worse.)

On Tiebreakers

Whenever two players who are trying for the same position appear to be equally good, the coaches will choose the player who stands better in the class-room. He is surer to be free of conditions when wanted, and his better head work counts in a game. Many a defeat may be attributed to slow thinking.

W. H. Lillard, *Football Rudiments*, 1911

Many a defeat? As many as slow running? Because I don't think it's as many as slow running. I am willing to bet a lot more defeats may be attributed to slow running.

VOL. LXXII. No. 1863.

PUCK BUILDING, New York, November 13th, 1912.

Copyright, 1912, by Keppler & Schwarzmann. Entered at N. Y. P. O. as Second-class Mail Matter.

PRICE TEN CENTS.

"What Fools these Mortals be"

Puck

"GEE, BUT YOU LOOK FUNNY!"

ON IMPLICATIONS

We have already shown how the ball may be carried by a player and how it may be kicked by him. Now he is permitted also to throw the ball forward, that is, toward the opponent's goal, under certain restrictions. He may always throw it back toward his own goal at any time. In the first place any man who wishes to make a forward pass must be at the time he makes it at least five yards back of his line of scrimmage, that is, as already described, the point where the ball was put in play.

WALTER CAMP, *FOOTBALL FOR THE SPECTATOR*, 1911

That's a pretty interesting difference between the game of 1911 and the one we know today. Another interesting difference is that you could stand two quarterbacks from 1911 directly on top of one another and they'd barely be tall enough to scratch Russell Wilson's backside. Kind of neat to think about.

On Sportsmanship

As to betting, President Draper says "that he once sat in a hotel lobby before a great game, and saw scores of boys from two leading American universities daring each other to put up money on their respective teams, and when the dare was accepted and the terms settled, as frequently happened, they placed their money in envelopes, which they gave to the clerk of the house, to be delivered to the winner after the game. The thing could hardly have been worse."

C. M. Woodward, *Opinions of Educators on the Value and Total Influence of Inter-Collegiate and Inter-Scholastic American Football as Played in 1903–1909*, 1910

In recent history, there have been multiple people decapitated when the soccer game they were officiating ended in a way that did not please both sides equally. So, I don't know, that friendly wager between adult amateurs maybe could have been slightly worse.

On Fool's Gold

Never be deceived into thinking a good run has been made when the man merely goes across the field. Many an otherwise good player loses his chance to get on a Varsity team from the fact that he runs too far across the field, or even runs back. It is the advance that counts and not the distance over which the runner passes, and the spectator should always bear this in mind, and he will not then make erroneous judgments about the quality of a man's playing.

Walter Camp and Lorin F. Deland, *Football*, 1896

This is honestly exhausting. You think the guy going backward is good? If it was good to go backward, we'd call it going forward! God!! We have like 400,000 more things to do and you're stuck on the going forward thing still!! Get a clue, dude!!!!!!

P
Q
30
10

On Roster Size

Twenty-five years of football, as player, fan and coach—and I'm not sure which description fits me best—have taught me first of all that the game is played not by eleven men but by eleven hundred or eleven thousand—by the whole student and graduate body of the institution, large or small, which those eleven men represent. This may sound like the loose and windy bombast of the all-too-common collegiate spellbinder, but . . .

William W. Roper, *Winning Football*, 1921

Correct. That is what it sounds like. The whole book sounds like this, actually. Surprised you didn't just stop here?

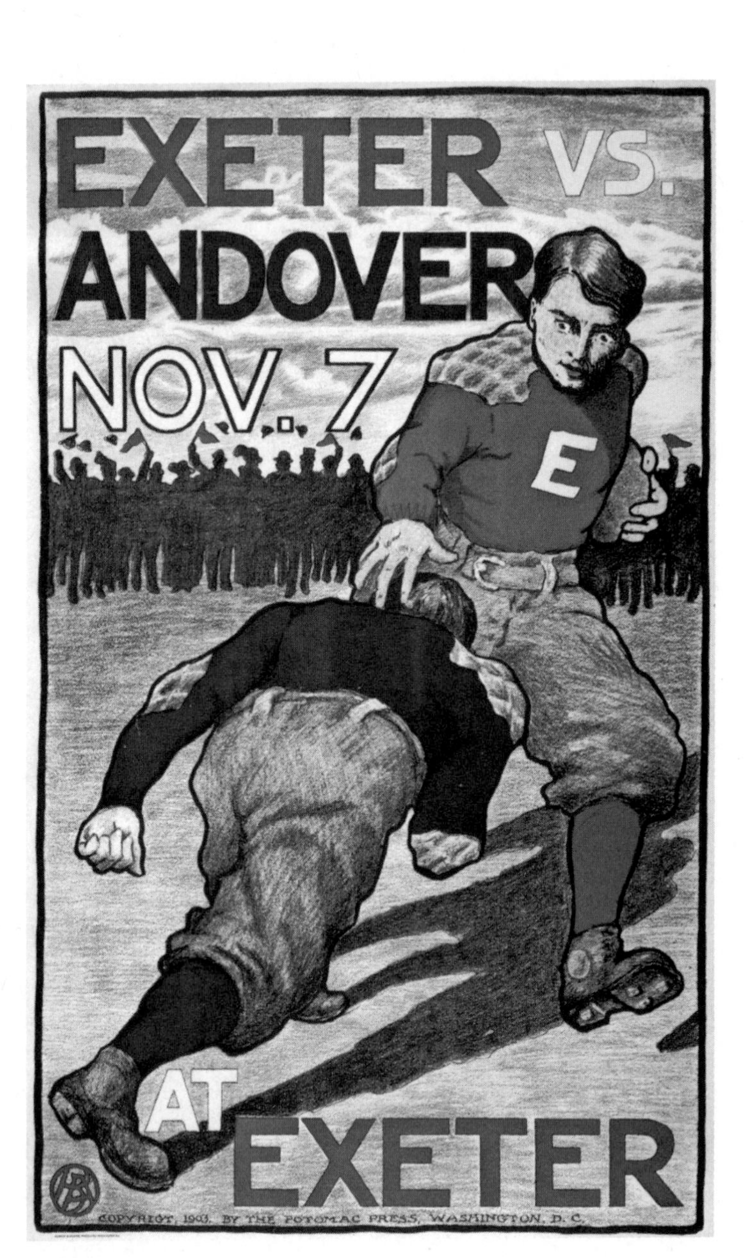
EXETER VS.
ANDOVER
NOV. 7
E
AT
EXETER
COPYRIGT, 1903. BY THE POTOMAC PRESS, WASHINGTON, D. C.

On Balance

With this diminution in the numbers a more open style of game naturally followed. . . . [P]layers were obliged to pick up the ball, and pass it with extreme quickness, and some of the best players were able to combine the two motions into one scoop. The advantages of dribbling were gradually felt to be important, and the forwards were required to be proficient in this respect also.

The Oxford Team and Short Passing. The Oxford team of 1882 was the first one to develop the art of passing to any great extent and as a result were victorious over the best clubs in the country during three successive seasons.

Walter Camp and Lorin F. Deland, *Football*, 1896

And one team, we gave 'em a bunch of knives, see, and they did pretty well! No other teams got knives, and they couldn't block the knives since they hadn't practiced against knives all year, so the knife team was, like, actually pretty dominant. Good group of guys. Called 'em the Knife Boys. Had to shut down after that, obviously, but it was a fun time in my life.

BROWN
B

On Purity, and Upstanding Moral Character, and Austerity, and . . .

There have been from time to time important movements looking toward the purification of football—commendably when the game was in dire straits. Not the least of these newer undertakings was the formation of the National Collegiate Athletic Association, and to its everlasting credit be it said that it began without ostentation or assumption of power, believing that "influence" and nothing else would justify its existence and the existence of the game it sought to some extent to guide but not control.

Herbert Reed, *Football For Public and Player*, 1913

HahahahahahahaHAHABWahahaHeheheh
[deep breath]
Gwaahhhaaahahahahahahhahahahahhhhuhuhuh
[choking]
Ha. Guide.

—Mae Goodelle Chaffee.

On Logyness

As for cream, nothing makes a man more logy. One can almost feel it choking his wind as it slides deliciously down the throat in its happy environment of strawberries or peaches. Milk, rather than cream, should by all means be served with cereals at a training table, and used, too, with the hot beverages permitted. Table water should be cooled in glass jars in the refrigerator, but not served with ice. The men should be discouraged from drinking while eating. Before and after the meal a glass of water is sufficient. While no serious harm may result from the moderate use of water during meals, the arguments against the practice are sufficiently strong to govern the man who is striving for the attainment of the highest form of physical excellence.

Maj. Frank W. Cavanaugh, *Inside Football*, 1919

But don't worry! Choking down this dry, powdery, pre-war chip beef on toast is so much fun you'll hardly have time to think about grasping desperately for literally any liquid that could potentially lubricate your starchy, cracked throat and keep you from choking to death on $0.35 worth of canned garbage.

Faneuil Hall
Old North Bridge
at Concord Mass
Christ
Church
LIQUID
GRANITE
A
BERRY BROTHERS
VARNISHES
State House
BOSTON
Old South Church

On the Sad and Precipitous Decline of Harvard

It is four years since football was abolished at Columbia, and there are now no undergraduates left there who have known or seen the demoralizing influence of intercollegiate football. It is the unanimous testimony of Columbia professors that the autumn weeks have now, for the first time, become quiet, orderly, and abundant in work. . . .

It is deplorable that Columbia's example has not been followed by other large institutions. President Eliot talked and thundered against football, but Harvard did not uphold him. . . . Columbia has gained for itself a proud pre-eminence by an act of conspicuous moral courage, good sense, and high intelligence.

Dr. Albert Shaw, *The American Review of Reviews*, 1909

If only Harvard had abolished football when it had the chance, perhaps it would not have faded into obscurity in the mid-1900s. As it is, we're left with the infamous provincial accent litmus, "I'm going to park the car on Boston College Yard."

"FOOTBALL & LOVE"
A STORY of THE
YALE-PRINCETON
GAME of '94 BY
Burr W. McIntosh
("TAFFY")
ILLUSTRATED BY B. WEST CLINEDINST.
DECORATIVE DESIGNS BY HOOPER
PRICE 50 CENTS.
THE TRANSATLANTIC PUBLISHING Co. 63 FIFTH AVENUE NEW YORK
26 HENRIETTA ST COVENT GARDEN LONDON
Hooper

On the West Coast Offense

On this basis the pass should be used for short as well as long gains. A running play that gains two and a half to three yards is regarded as successful. Why should not the pass be used in the same way? Passes that give little or no gain in themselves, but put the receiver in position for open field running, and at least a few yards gain, disorganize the defense, eventually make the long passes successful, spread the defense so bucking becomes possible, and contribute generally to making the forward pass a regular ground gaining play—a part of the regular attack.

Elmer Berry, *The Forward Pass in Football*, 1921

It's impossible for a number of reasons, but this reads so much like a fan trying to talk himself into Sam Bradford being good that it no longer matters what it actually is.

On Technique

There are several types of charge for the offensive line man. He may drive ahead with his shoulder, holding his forearms and elbows in front of his stomach. He may drive ahead with one elbow advanced and re-enforced by locked hands. Either of these methods may be used, either driving straight into the opponent or by dipping well under him. Should the defensive line man dive head-on under the play, the offensive line man must either walk on and over him or dip his leg under the dive before it gets to the ground. Once an offensive line man gets his knees under the shoulders of his opponent he can often walk him straight to the rear.

Charles D. Daly, *American Football*, 1921

Oh, so we can lock our arms, drive our elbows straight into our opponents' heads, and then either step on them or trip them with our spiked shoes? And a lot of people died on the field while this sport was being developed, you say? Well, doesn't that beat all!

But this shows a genuine tackle. In approaching from the runner's right side the tackler has thrust his head and shoulders in front of the runner and is using his arms like a vise to hold the man tight while he drives him backward. Note that the tackler's right foot is planted *near the runner*. This is very important, for it makes possible a gain of one or two yards by the defensive side. And inches count!

Also, the runner is now carrying the ball properly (both ends locked securely) with the nearer hand available in his attempt to elude the tackler.

On Perfect Form

But this shows a genuine tackle. In approaching from the runner's right side the tackler has thrust his head and shoulders in front of the runner and is using his arms like a vise to hold the man tight while he drives him backward. Note that the tackler's right foot is planted near the runner. This is very important, for it makes possible a gain of one or two yards by the defensive side. And inches count!

Also, the runner is now carrying the ball properly (both ends locked securely) with the nearer hand available in his attempt to elude the tackler.

W. H. Lillard, *Football Rudiments*, 1911

It's not a "genuine tackle" unless you slam your neck into the runner's knees at full speed, snapping your spine like a Ritz cracker and allowing him to stomp a hole in your lifeless body on his way to the end zone.

On Civilization

> Of all the games played in the civilized world the most execrable is American football, nor is there anything more unintelligible than the fascination which this brutal and degrading pastime has for an intelligent nation like the Americans. . . . Things have come to such a pass this year that, although the season is comparatively young, a dozen or more "football deaths" have already been recorded. I am glad to hear that, as the result of the death of one of its cadets, football at West Point Academy has been stopped, and I hope that this may prove the beginning of the end of a game which is a disgrace to modern civilization.
>
> "Chartered Hooliganism," *The Bystander, ca. 1907*

Yeah, that would be terrible if the young men who signed up to go to college at West Point ended up dying in a conflict of some kind. Now to look up what a "service academy" is and map out the next eight years of Archduke Franz Ferdinand's life while drinking a large cup of terrible twentieth-century coffee.

On Decision Trees

> When the ball in a succession of plays of this varying character is so held by a team as to be within possible kicking distance of the goal, they may, instead of trying further running plays, determine that it is better policy to try what is called a field kick at the goal.
>
> Walter Camp, *Football For The Spectator*, 1911

They may also, in the course of navigating the opportunity, decide to affix their gaze on a very large and complicated placard for such a time that executing a play before the play clock has expired will be impossible, thereby forcing the use of a precious timeout, after which any momentum will be lost and ultimately another option altogether is selected. This sequence is formally known as "Reiding the defense."

Copyright 1906
Celebrity Art

On Equanimity

The coaching, practicing and playing of a picked team stands in the way of general athletics. Only a small minority of the student body participates in such games with sufficient regularity to reap the benefit which may come to the steady player. Not 10 per cent of the students play on a large school or college team long enough to get the good things I have named; on the contrary, a few picked boys or men dominate everything for three months every year.

C. M. Woodward, *Opinions of Educators on the Value and Total Influence of Inter-Collegiate and Inter-Scholastic American Football as Played in 1903–1909*, 1910

Good point. How many students are in Chemistry 201 on MWF at 10:30 a.m. (lab Thursdays at noon)? Like thirty? What is that, 0.1 percent of the college or so? Yeah, let's ban that. And I'm not just saying that because I got a C in it, either. I really, uh, believe in the cause . . . or whatever.

CLEAR

On Conditioning

Physical condition must be at its best for a team to win. This is not easy to secure, but it is by no means the most difficult part of the season's work, if the men live right. The work should be regulated very carefully throughout the season and the men should not find the physical side of their work too much. They should not feel exhausted and "all in" at night and after the first ten days the soreness and stiffness should be gone from the muscles.

John R. Richards, *Inside Dope on Football Coaching*, 1917

Hey, cool, it's day eight. Just two more days of concentrated swelling in the muscles caused by infinitesimal tears and other damage to fibrous and membranous tissues in my body's discrete muscle groups, resulting in the release of molecular irritants that easily bind to pain receptors in my brain and register the same electrical signature as "burning," because that stuff only happens for ten days and not forever. Phew.

On Cromulence

Not the least of the goodly football influences have been such men as Dean Briggs of Harvard, elected in 1912 president of the National Collegiate Athletic Association, and men like Dr. A. L. Sharpe, of Yale, who took upon himself the recrudescence of Cornell football in more ways than one, not to mention other semi-athletes, semi-faculty men, whose word is accepted alike by the athletic element and the gentlemen of the university staff.

Herbert Reed, *Football For Public and Player*, 1913

Well, considering how cruddy Cornell football has been this past century, I'd say he did a damn good job!

FOOT-
BALL.
A. Alford.

On Assuming Nothing

DRILLS

There are two drills in connection with the forward pass which should be practiced throughout the season:

PASSING

The passer, with receivers and substitutes, should assemble at the various critical positions on the field and the passer should practice throwing the ball on his different plays to the various receivers...

Charles D. Daly, *American Football*, 1921

Whoa, whoa, slow down, pal! Remember, I'm a rookie here, so let's start with the basics. First up: Where did we come from, why are we here, who am I, why don't they make the $1 coins anymore, is the moon my friend, why do I have to wash out my recyclables when they're just going to the dump anyway, and do dogs have souls? Answer those and we'll talk about your precious drills, whatever they are.

On the Dangers of Mobility

Passing to the side flat, in rear of, or along, the rush line is highly dangerous. Passing to the territory uncovered by a charging tackle or end, if the pass is made directly ahead, is however, sometimes effective. The best passes are made to the receiver going to the open spaces down field. The receiver reaches this space by change of direction and pace, and he takes the ball going fast, generally turned in.

Passes cannot be made on the run.

Charles D. Daly, *American Football*, 1921

Oh yeah, definitely don't run while throwing the football. You might accidentally become the MVP of the regular season and of Super Bowl XXIX, setting records for most points scored and most touchdowns thrown in the process, while also nabbing a fifth championship for your team and guaranteeing your spot in the Pro Football Hall of Fame.

Just throw it the normal way.

JOHN E Sheridan

On Uniformity

> In the first place, the uniforms, which would hardly attract attention save as rather soiled and badly fitting garments, are the product of considerable study. The original uniform consisted of tight-fitting jerseys, and tight, as well as rather thin, knickerbockers. There was no padding whatever, and nothing to break the force of falls. The first step in reform was the adoption of the canvas jacket worn over the jersey. . . . The next reform in uniforms was in the line of padding, and the trousers or knickerbockers we see to-day are practically loose bags heavily padded at the knees and thighs. Padding is also being used more or less in the jackets and jerseys. There are also many appliances in the way of shin guards, nose guards, and other parts of armor, but there is a rule that forbids the use of any metal substance on the person of the player, so that such armor as is used is supposed to be of a material that will not injure the opponents. There are also individual appliances of all kinds, both as a prevention and as a cure of injuries,—ankle supporters, knee caps, and the like.
>
> Walter Camp and Lorin F. Deland, *Football*, 1896

And the best part of all this—out of the whole uniform and padding thing—is that, by putting all of these elements between players and their bodies, essentially emphasizing these points of constant contact, and removing players from the consequences of their physical actions, we're making the game SAFER, and not incredibly, irresponsibly dangerous. Cool, right?

On Athleticism by Osmosis

Sometimes I hear well-meaning people—even people who know a little about the surface of the game itself—speak slightingly of this enthusiasm. Side-line and grand-stand spirit, they call it, and if it were true that such an atmosphere bred a tendency to take one's own exercise on the bleachers, I should agree with them in part at least. But I find it strongly effective in exactly the opposite direction. The more I can rouse football enthusiasm in a man utterly unable to play the game, the easier it becomes to persuade that man to develop his body and to keep it in decent running repair.

William W. Roper, *Winning Football*, 1921

Of course, which is why the stereotype of the lightning-quick, phenomenally muscular football fan with an arm like a cannon and a perfect understanding of complex football strategy endures to this very day!

On Turnips

The training table should supply all the vegetables, excepting turnips, carefully cooked and properly served. Vegetables should feature especially at the evening meal, when by their use the men may avoid the error of consuming too much meat. Men can digest more meat during the football season than at other times, but they will be better off if they consume comparatively small quantities of it at the evening meal. However, the backbone of the training table is its liberal supply of high-grade lamb and beef, chops and steaks.

Maj. Frank W. Cavanaugh, *Inside Football*, 1919

This is the first and only mention of turnips in *Inside Football.* At no point is it ever explained why turnips should not be served at the training table, or if they should be consumed at all, by football players or otherwise. Seriously, "turnip" never appears again in the text. Look it up yourself. It's insane.

University of Florida

On Salaries

The spirit of the best kind of amateur—that of sport for sport's sake—inevitably suffers under a system where each team is made up of the obedient tools of a highly-paid professional. Under such a system, contests tend to degenerate into the triumph of this or that coach. The Committee are also convinced that the paying of great sums of money to men who instruct our youths in what should be, not their work, but their play, tends to vitiate the opinion not only of the student body, but of the whole community, as to what is of real importance in a college training and in the education of a young man.

A. C. Coolidge, Chairman of the Athletic Committee at Harvard, ca. 1905

If you're reading this right now and you're one of the people who thinks it's fair for college players to not be paid while universities, leagues, and networks make billions off their likenesses and performances, you have got to feel pretty damn stupid! This guy knew we had to pay the players only about eight years after the ice cream scoop was invented.

PUCK BUILDING, New York, September 24th, 1913.

VOL. LXXIV. No. 1908.

PRICE TEN CENTS.

WHEN DUTY CALLS.

THE SPARTAN MOTHER.—Go, my boy!

On Nationalism

There is a distinctive flavor about an Army-Navy football game which, irrespective of the quality of the contending elevens and of their relative standing among the high-class teams in any given season, rates these contests annually as among the "big games" of the year. Tactically and strategically football bears a close relation to war. That is a vital reason why it should be studied and applied in our two government schools.

[F]ootball in its essence is a stern, grim game, a game that calls for self-sacrifice, for mental alertness and for endurance; all these are elements, among others, which we commonly associate with the soldier's calling.

William H. Edwards, *Football Days: Memories of the Game and of the Men behind the Ball*, 1916

This was published in the middle of World War I, which means this guy took one look at tanks, flamethrowers, and trenches full of mustard gas and went, "Oh yeah, that's like when the running back scores a touchdown." What the hell, man??

The Other Professional Football Leagues and How They Met Their Demise

- **XFL**
  Vince McMahon. Well, okay, maybe it's not that simple. Despite a few memorable traits that would later be adopted by the NFL (the Sunday Night Football signature Sky Cam chief among them), the XFL was a conceptual mishmash that never seemed certain how much was acceptable to lift from its spiritual ancestor, professional wrestling.
- **USFL**
  Well, when you put an egomaniacal, self-aggrandizing, silver-spooned fake billionaire in charge and give him carte blanche to play negotiator despite ample evidence he is either incapable or unwilling to act like anything approaching a rational or sympathetic person, what do you expect to happen? Luckily, we all learned our lesson after that.
- **UFL**
  Former Wall Street banker teams up with wealthy politician to spend eight figures for a trophy named after himself. Being late with payments to players and an absurdly short season probably didn't help, either. At least they got overtime right.
- **AFL**
  "Demise" might be too strong to describe what happened to the AFL, but it used to exist and now it doesn't, so it really depends on your perspective. A Buddhist might say the AFL is now the most powerful league in the world; more likely he would say "What is football?" but that's a different book.

- **NFL Europe**
  Here's one league that really should be resurrected somehow, if not for its entertainment value, then at least for its utility. Comprised of two eras over a sixteen-year period, NFL Europe served as the NFL's only official development league, and was legitimately successful as a talent pool for both players (Kurt Warner, Jake Delhomme) and broadcasters (Troy Aikman, Curt Menefee). But the benefits were not tangible enough for the NFL to continue to absorb the losses in TV revenue and operating costs attributable to the league's over-concentration in Germany and sporadic sponsorships. And with the NCAA content to operate as a complementary marketing arm and development league in its own right, what's the point of shipping potential stars across the Atlantic where they can't be monetized?

- **Arena Football League**
  This version of the AFL is currently operating, so its inclusion on this list is as placeholder only. At press time, the league had been dissolved more than Alka-Seltzer, so who knows what's next for these crazy kids? Running full speed into a wall and flipping over it into the crowd would be my guess.

- **af2**
  The Arena Football League's developmental league. Come on, there's no way this was going to work. I mean, I know it did for a decade, but really? The Oklahoma City Yard Dawgz? It was a matter of time. Do not shed a tear for af2.

- **All the rest**
  The AAFC, some other AFLs, the CFL (not that one), the FXFL, the IFL, the PSFL, a bunch of others . . . they probably stunk. I mean, right? I don't know. Never saw 'em.

On Blank Verses

The bard of Avon, unless he should be indulging in the license of anachronism, would give the game a place even among the Ephesians, for does not Dromio in Scene I of Act II of the "Comedy of Errors" ask Adriana:

"Am I so round with you as you with me,
That like a football you do spurn me thus?"

Parke H. Davis, *Football: The American Intercollegiate Game*, 1917

Footballs aren't round, they're oblong! If this kind of accuracy is par for the course, it's no wonder I never knew that Akon's Band did comedy.

FRANK A NANKIVELL

On Inflation

RULE II

Ball

Section 1. The ball shall be made of leather, enclosing a rubber bladder. It shall be tightly inflated and shall have the shape of a prolate spheroid—Circumference, long axis, from 28 inches to 28 ½ inches; short axis from 22 ½ to 23 inches; weight, from 14 ounces to 15 ounces.

John R. Richards, *Inside Dope on Football Coaching*, 1917

NOTE: If you're a real handsome MVP-type quarterback in a cold weather city, don't worry about this stuff too much. It's more like guidelines than anything else; suggestions, really. You know what works best for you. Sometimes that's gonna be following the rulebook to the letter like everyone else, and sometimes it's gonna be a purposefully smashed cell phone. Who's to say, really, except scientists, your employers, your accomplices, etc.

Bristow Adams.
ANNAPOLIS
COPYRIGHT 1902 BY THE POTOMAC PRESS, WASHINGTON, D. C.

On Tea Leaves

> It is not always easy even for the umpire to be sure when a side is going to kick the ball. They may kick it on the first down, the second down, or the third down. Of course, a great many kicks are made on the third down, because that is the last chance, but it is now by no means unusual in good teams to see kicks made much earlier than that.
>
> Walter Camp and Lorin F. Deland, *Football*, 1896

It wouldn't even be completely unthinkable for a team to kick it on every possession, regardless of field position or game situation. Just kick, kick, kick—kicking all the time. Bunch of guys who either don't like football or think they're playing something else, or maybe they're just goofing off . . . not sure. They can just kick it all the livelong day, nothing ever being accomplished. The other team is totally confused. Great sport we got here. Hope it never changes.

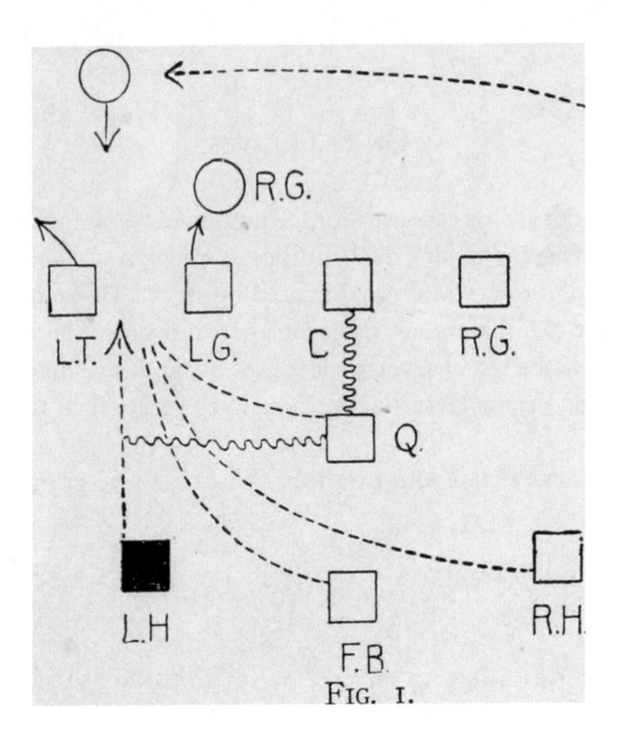

FIG. I.

ON MINIMALISM

An analysis of the foregoing will show that a well-rounded attack should have eight running plays (four or five of which can be executed from open formation), a kick, three passes (one to the center and one to either flank), and one or two standard deceptions, one of which is the fake kick. Under no circumstances should there be more than these fourteen plays. If the character of the team and its development permit, the number may be reduced.

CHARLES D. DALY, *AMERICAN FOOTBALL*, 1921

"No team will ever need more than fourteen plays" is a demonstrably bad prediction. "If they master those fourteen, the coach can shrink the playbook a bit" is just trolling.

On Advanced Military Tactics

It was Wellington, was it not, who said that the battle of Waterloo had been won on the cricket fields of Eton, and it might well be prophesied of our next war that it will be won on the football fields of our schools and universities.

Herbert Reed, *Football for Public and Player*, 1913

(It wasn't.)

On Familiar Profanity

Five or six years ago I had occasion to leave my home early on the morning after Thanksgiving to meet an engagement at a teachers' association. On the way the football team from one of the central and conspicuous high schools of the country who had been out to play a Thanksgiving game, came into the car on their way home. They had been victorious, and their conduct was beyond description. Boys of the high school age, who manifestly lived in respectable homes, seemed to think it manly to indulge in profanity and obscenity with a familiarity which was shocking. They passed a bottle of liquor from one to another, and when the train stopped went out to have it refilled. The conditions were appalling and most suggestive.

C. M. Woodward, *Opinions of Educators on the Value and Total Influence of Inter-Collegiate and Inter-Scholastic American Football as Played in 1903–1909*, 1910

Will someone please invite this man to a party? Good god. He's more uptight than the rich socialite lady at the beginning of a rap video.

F. EARL CHRISTY

On Hardening Men

One of the commonest methods of hardening men in the old times—and it has stubbornly clung to a place in even modern practice—was the grand old plan of falling on the ball. I think that every squad in the country spent more of its first few days in this particular exercise than in anything else. One reason for it probably lay in the beautiful ease with which any volunteer coach, with a leathern lung and an uninventive brain, could put the neophyte through it, bawling lustily at him as his tender-skinned body slid over the rasping turf. Perhaps it was fun, too, for those who didn't have to do it. It amused the bleachers to see the antics of beginners and there was some pleasure in it for the adept who could cover the ball like a hen with a lonesome chicken, but I can see no other excuse for it, then or now.

William W. Roper, *Winning Football*, 1921

Honestly, the drill wouldn't be so bad if it weren't for all the lusty bawling over my tender skin. Sliding over the rasping turf? Fine. Covering the ball like a hen with a lonesome chicken? Not bad at all. But the lusty bawling . . . no thank you.

PRINCETON
H.G. LASKEY

On Kick Wisdom

There is one point to be remembered in this connection, and that is, that the side in possession of the ball, having made two of these attempts without success, usually prefers to forego a third at running advance, and instead of this, to kick the ball as far down the field as possible, rather than by the third attempt to surrender it at the spot where they failed to their opponents. The wisdom of such a course is patent, for a kick will send a ball some fifty yards into the opposing territory, and thus start the opponents at a comfortable distance away from the goal they wish to reach.

Walter Camp, *Football For The Spectator*, 1911

They had three downs back then, instead of four. But millennials are lazy?? Hmmmm . . .

FOOT BALL.

On Dessert

For desserts, puddings and fruit salads are safest things to offer. As a general rule, the ban on pie and other lard-made pastry should very seldom be lifted. Plain cake, however, follows only the rule for bread; when new-made it is unfit for consumption. Many trainers will serve cottage pudding whose hands go up in horror at the mention of cake. Cottage pudding plainly implies cake, and the material used in this confection should stand at least twenty-four hours after the original baking. Indian pudding, bread pudding, corn starch, tapioca, rice and custards are recommended, and ice cream may be served occasionally for variety. Nuts and raisins also provide a welcome relief in the dreary wilderness of puddings.

Maj. Frank W. Cavanaugh, *Inside Football*, 1919

My Dearest Martha,

This is to be my final testament. How long it has been since my most recent letter I can only guess, so confounding have the intervening days in this opaque and creamy hellscape been to me. I do know that I have not seen so much as the specter of a nut or raisin since the custard rains passed, and even in those days the ice cream was as bitter as ink and twice as thick. I miss you dreadfully, Martha. If I shall ever escape this swirling pudding madness, I should endeavor to make you my wife. With God's grace and more luck than I deserve, that day will be soon.

Yours Sweetly,

Clarence "The Spoonman" Starchly IV

On Fumble Recovery

A proper recovery of a loose ball. The player not only has the ball beyond question, but he is also in a safe position to receive a ton of rivals. Note that he has really fallen around the ball rather than on it.

W. H. Lillard, *Football Rudiments*, 1911

Note also that the player appears to be crying. Boohooing, wailing, gnashing teeth, caterwauling, and bellyaching are all crucial components of the ideal fumble recovery. The more distraught you are while scooping up the bouncing, cartwheeling ball, the better.

Acknowledgments

Thank you to my wife, Alicia, and my mother, Betsy, for being so supportive of my nonsense.

Also, to David J. Roth for believing and, more importantly, saying that I am a good writer.

Finally, to my daughters Ellie and Keely, who didn't really do anything at all for this book and, in fact, can't even read it yet.